KNITTING & CROCHET
BABIES' CLOTHES

Marshall Cavendish

CONTENTS

Published by Marshall Cavendish Books Limited
58 Old Compton Street
London W1V 5PA

© Marshall Cavendish Limited 1976 – 84

Printed and bound in Italy by
New Interlitho SpA.

First printing 1976
This printing 1984

ISBN 0 86307 212 7

This volume is not to be sold in Australia,
New Zealand or North America

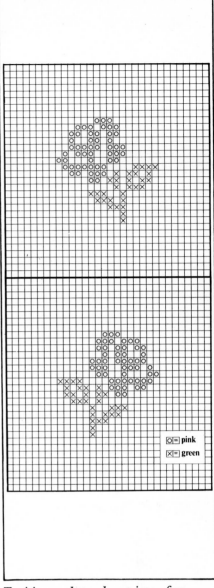

○== pink
×=== green

Tunisian crochet makes up into a firm, fairly bulky fabric which is just right for a cosy pram blanket. The flowers are worked in Swiss darning (see graph for positioning).

Tunisian crochet pram blanket

Size
80cm *(31½in)* x 60cm *(23½in)*
Tension
18 sts and 16 pairs of rows to 10cm *(3.9in)* over patt worked on No.4.00 (ISR) Tunisian hook
Materials
12 x 25grm balls Hayfield Beaulon Crepe Double Knitting in main shade, A
2 balls of contrast colour, B
1 ball or oddments of contrast colour, C

One No.4.00 (ISR) Tunisian crochet hook
One No.3.50 (ISR) crochet hook

First square
Using No.4.00 (ISR) Tunisian hook and A, make 36ch.
1st row Insert hook into 2nd ch from hook, yrh and draw a loop through the ch, *insert hook into next ch, yrh and draw a loop through, rep from * to end. Do not turn. 36 loops on hook.
2nd row Working from left to right, yrh and draw through first loop on hook, *yrh and draw through 2 loops, rep from * to end. Do not turn.
3rd row *Insert hook from right to left behind vertical loop of next st, yrh and draw a loop through, rep from * to end. Do not turn. 36 loops on hook.

4th row As 2nd.
Rep 3rd and 4th rows 14 times more.
Fasten off.
Make 11 more squares in the same way.
Work roses in cross stitch from chart, alternating the two motifs on the squares.

To make up
Using No.3.50 (ISR) hook and B, join squares with dc into a rectangle of 4 squares long and 3 squares wide.
Edging Using No.3.50 (ISR) hook, B and with RS of work facing, work a row of dc all round blanket. Join with a ss into first dc. Turn. Work a second row of dc with WS of work facing. Join with a ss into first st. Fasten off.
Press lightly under a dry cloth with a cool iron.

1

Lace jacket bonnet & bootees

Sizes
To fit 46cm *(18in)* chest
Jacket length to shoulder, 23cm *(9in)*
Sleeve seam, 12cm *(4¾in)*
Tension
3 patts to 11cm *(4¼in)* in width and 12

rows to 10cm *(3.9in)* over main patt worked on No.2.50 (ISR) crochet hook
Materials
6 x 20grm balls Sunbeam Tricel Nylon Knit & Crochet 4 ply
One No.2.50 (ISR) crochet hook
One pair No.12 needles
2 metres *(1.80 yards)* ribbon

Jacket
Using No.2.50 (ISR) hook make 73ch and beg at neck edge.
1st row Into 4th ch from hook work 1tr, (1tr into each of next 10ch, 3tr into next ch) twice, 1tr into each of next 23ch, 3tr into

This charming set for a new baby consists of a ribbon-trimmed matinee jacket, bonnet and bootees.

next ch, 1tr into each of next 10ch, 3tr into next ch, 1tr into each of next 12ch. Turn. 79tr.
2nd row 3ch to count as first tr, (1tr into each of next 12tr, 3tr into next tr) twice, 1tr into each of next 25tr, (3tr into next tr, 1tr into each of next 12tr) twice, 1tr into 3rd of 3ch. Turn. 87tr.
3rd row 3ch, 1tr into each of next 13tr, 3tr into next tr, 1tr into each of next 14tr, 3tr into next tr, 1tr into each of next 27tr,

3tr into next tr, 1tr into each of next 14tr,
3tr into next tr, 1tr into each of next 13tr,
1tr into 3rd of 3ch. Turn. 95tr.
4th row 3ch, 1tr into each of next 14tr,
3 tr into next tr, 1tr into each of next 16tr,
3tr into next tr, 1tr into each of next 29tr,
3tr into next tr, 1tr into each of next 16tr,
3tr into next tr, 1tr into each of next 14tr,
1tr into 3rd of 3ch. Turn. 103tr.
5th row 3ch, miss next tr, *(1tr, 2ch, 1tr)
into next tr – called V st –, miss 2tr, 7tr
into next tr, miss 3tr, rep from * to last
3 sts, V st into next tr, miss 1tr, 1tr into 3rd
of 3ch. Turn. 14½ patts = 15 V sts and 14
7tr gr.
6th row 3ch, *3tr into V st, 1tr into 2nd of
7tr, (1ch, 1tr into next tr) 4 times, rep from
* to last V st, 3tr into V st, 1tr into 3rd of
3ch. Turn.
7th row 3ch, *1tr into each of next 4tr,
(1tr in to 1ch sp, 1tr into next tr) 4 times,
rep from * to last 4 sts, 1tr into each of
next 3tr, 1tr into 3rd of 3ch. Turn. 173tr.
8th row Work in tr, inc 2 sts at each
raglan. 181tr.
Work 2 more rows in tr, dec one st at
centre back of 2nd of these rows. 180tr.
11th row As 5th. 25½ patts = 26 V sts and
25 7tr gr.
12th row As 6th .
13th row 3ch, miss 1tr, *V st into next tr,
miss 3tr, 7tr into next tr, miss 3tr, rep from
* ending with V st into next tr, miss 1tr,
1tr into 3rd of 3ch. Turn.
14th row As 6th.
15th row Work over 4 patts, miss next 5
patts for sleeve, work over next 7½ patts,
miss next 5 patts for second sleeve, work
over last 4 patts. Turn.
Cont on these 15½ patts for back and fronts
for a further 13 rows. Fasten off.
With RS of work facing, rejoin yarn to 5
patts missed for sleeves and patt 12 rows.
Fasten off.
Cuffs
Using No.12 needles and with RS of work
facing, K up 43 sts along edge of sleeve.
1st row P1, *K1, P1, rep from * to end.
2nd row K1, *P1, K1, rep from * to end.
Rep last 2 rows until cuff measures 4cm
(1½in) from beg. Cast off in rib.
Edging
Using No.2.50 (ISR) hook and with RS of
work facing, rejoin yarn to lower right
front corner, 2ch, 3tr into same place,
*miss 1 row end, work (1dc, 2ch, 3tr) into
next row end, rep from * up right front,
round neck and down left front. Fasten off.

To make up
Do not press. Join sleeve seams. Thread
ribbon through 2nd row of tr at neck. If
necessary, press seams under a dry cloth
with a cool iron.

Bonnet
Using No.2.50 (ISR) hook make 5ch. Join
with a ss into first ch to form a circle.
1st round 3ch to count as first tr, 13tr into
circle. Join with a ss into 3rd of 3ch. 14 sts.
2nd round 3ch, 1tr into same place, 2tr

into each tr to end. Join with a ss into 3rd
of 3ch. 28 sts.
3rd round 3ch, 2tr into next tr, *1tr into
next tr, 2tr into next tr, rep from * to end.
Join with a ss into 3rd of 3ch. 42 sts.
4th round 3ch, 1tr into each of next 3tr,
*2tr into next tr, 1tr into each of next 2tr,
rep from * to last 2tr, 1tr into each of next
2tr. Join with a ss into 3rd of 3ch. 54 sts.
5th round 3ch, miss 1tr, *V st into next tr,
miss 2tr, 7tr into next tr, miss 3tr, rep from
* 6 times more, V st into next tr, miss 1tr,
1tr into next tr. Do not join, but turn work
and cont in rows. 7½ patts.
5th row As 6th row of jacket.
Rep 2 patt rows 7 times more. Fasten off.
Edging
Turn last 4 patt rows to RS of work. Using
No.2.50 (ISR) hook and with RS of work
facing, beg at front of lower edge and work
an odd number of dc round neck edge.
Turn.
Next row 4ch to count as first tr and ch,
miss next dc, *1tr into next dc, 1ch, miss
next dc, rep from * ending with 1tr into
last dc. Fasten off.
Thread ribbon through holes at neck.

Bootees
Using No.2.50 (ISR) hook make 32ch.
1st row Into 4th ch from hook work 1tr,
1tr into each ch to end. Turn. 30tr.
Work 2 more rows in tr. Fasten off.
Next row Miss 11tr, rejoin yarn to next tr,
3ch, 1tr into each of next 7tr, turn.
Work 4 more rows on these 8tr, dec one st
in centre of last row. 7tr. Fasten off.
Next row With RS of work facing, rejoin
yarn at beg of 11 missed tr, 3ch, V st into
next tr, miss 2tr, 7tr into next tr, miss 2tr,
V st into next tr, miss 2tr, 7tr into next tr,
cont along side of foot, miss 2 rows, V st
into next row, miss 2 rows, 7tr into corner,
V st into centre tr of toe, 7tr into corner,
cont along other side of foot, miss 2 rows,
V st into next row, miss 2 rows, 7tr into
next tr, miss 2tr, V st into next tr, miss
2tr, 7tr into next tr, miss 2tr, V st into next
tr, 1tr into last tr. Turn. 6½ patts.
Patt 3 rows.
Next row 3ch, (miss 1 st, 1tr into next st)
twice, 1tr into each of next 30 sts, (miss 1 st,
1tr into next st) 4 times, 1tr into each of
next 30 sts, (miss 1 st, 1tr into next st)
twice. Turn. 69tr.
Next row 3ch, (miss 1tr, 1tr into next tr)
twice, 1tr into each of next 26tr, (miss 1tr,
1tr into next tr) 4 times, 1tr into each of
next 26tr, (miss 1tr, 1tr into next tr) twice.
Turn. 61tr.
Next row 3ch, (miss 1tr, 1tr into next tr)
twice, 1tr into each of next 22tr, (miss 1tr,
1tr into next tr) 4 times, 1tr into each of
next 22tr, (miss 1tr, 1tr into next tr) twice.
Fasten off.

To make up
Work edging as given for jacket round top
of bootee. Join back seam and seam under
foot. Thread ribbon through 3rd row of tr
from beg.

Striped crochet pram bag

Sizes
To fit 46–51cm *(18–20in)* chest
Length, 70cm *(27½in)*
Tension
19tr and 10 rows to 10cm *(3.9in)* over tr
worked on No.3.50 (ISR) hook
Materials
2 x 50grm balls Madame Pingouin in each of
8 colours, A, B, C, D, E, F, G and H
One No.3.50 (ISR) crochet hook
61cm *(24in)* zip fastener

Back
Using No.3.50 (ISR) hook and A, make
90ch.
1st row Into 4th ch from hook work 1tr,
1tr into each ch to end. Turn. 88tr.
2nd row 3ch to count as first tr, 1tr into
each tr, ending with last tr into 3rd of 3ch.
Turn. Break off yarn.
Rep 2nd row throughout, working 2 rows
each in B, C, D, E, F, G, H and A until 38
rows have been completed. Dec one st at
each end of next and every foll alt row until
68tr rem, *at the same time* after 48 rows
from beg have been completed, cont in
same stripe sequence but working one row
only in each colour until 60 rows have been
completed from beg.
Shape armholes
Next row Miss 4 sts, join E to next st, 3ch,
patt to last 4 sts, turn. Break off E.
Next row Miss 3 sts, join F to next st, 3ch,
patt to last 3 sts, turn. Break off F.
Next row Miss first st, join G to next st,
3ch, patt to last st, turn. Break off G.
Next row Using H, work as given for last
row. 50tr.
Cont in stripe sequence, work 4 rows
without shaping.
Shape neck
Next row Using E, 3ch, 1tr into each of
next 16tr, work 2tr tog, turn.
Next row Using F, 3ch, work 2tr tog, patt
to end. Turn.
Next row Using G, 3ch, 1tr into each of
next 14tr, work 2tr tog. Fasten off.
Miss 12tr in centre for back neck, rejoin E
to next st, 3ch, work 2tr tog, patt to end.
Complete to match first side.

Left front
Using No.3.50 (ISR) hook and A, make
46ch. Work 1st–2nd rows as given for back.
44tr. Cont in patt as given for back until
38 rows have been completed from beg.
Dec one st at beg of next and every foll alt
row until 34tr rem. Cont without shaping
until 60 rows have been completed from
beg.
Shape armhole
Next row Miss 4 sts, join E to next st, 3ch,
patt to end. Turn.
Next row Using F, 3ch, patt to last 3 sts,

3

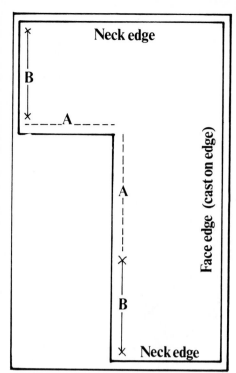

Above : Diagram for making up hood. 1. Join A to A. 2. Join B to B. 3. Slip stitch neck edge of hood to neck edge of pram bag.

37ch. Work 1st row as given for back. 35tr. Cont in tr, working 1 row in each colour and inc one st at each end of 3rd and every foll 3rd row until there are 47 sts. Cont without shaping until 20 rows have been completed from beg.

Shape top

Next row Miss 3 sts, join E to next st, 3ch, patt to last 3 sts, turn.
Dec 2 sts at each end of next row and one st at each end of foll row. Rep last 2 rows twice more. Dec 2 sts at each end of next 3 rows, ending with a stripe in F. Fasten off.

Hood

Using No.3.50 (ISR) hook and A, make 71ch. Work 1st row as given for back. 69tr.
Cont in tr, working 1 row in each colour until 20 rows have been completed from beg.

Next row Using E, 3ch, 1tr into each of of next 28tr, turn.
Cont on these 29tr, work 1 row each in F, G, F and E. Fasten off.

To make up

Do not press. Join shoulder seams. Set in sleeves. Join side and sleeve seams. Join hood as shown in diagram, then sew to neck edge. Using No.3.50 (ISR) hook, C and with RS of work facing work a row of dc (working approx 2dc into each row end) up right front, round hood and down left front, turn and work a second row. Using C, work 2 rows dc round lower edge of sleeves. Sew in zip, placing top of zip to neck edge. Join lower part of front seam as far as zip. Join lower edge of bag. Make a twisted cord using A and thread through first 1 row stripe in A at waist.

turn.
Cont in stripe sequence, dec one st at armhole edge on next 2 rows. 25tr. Work 1 row.

Shape neck

Next row (WS) Miss 4 sts, join B to next st, 3ch, patt to end. Turn.
Next row Using C, patt to last 2 sts, turn.
Next row Miss 2 sts, join D to next st, 3ch, patt to end. Turn.
Cont in stripe sequence, dec one st at neck edge on next row. 16tr. Work 3 rows,

Simple trebles worked in five colours make up this zipped pram bag with drawstring waist.

ending with a stripe in H. Fasten off.

Right front

Work to match left front, reversing all shaping.

Sleeves

Using No.3.50 (ISR) hook and A, make

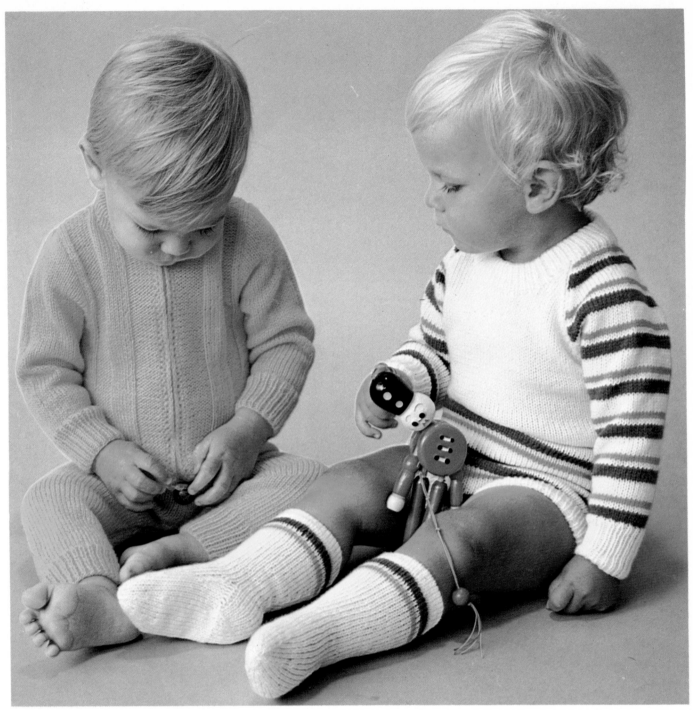

Knitted one~piece suit

Sizes
To fit 46cm (*18in*) chest
Length from shoulder to ankle, 58cm (*22¾in*)
Sleeve seam, 19cm (*7½in*)

Tension
28 sts and 36 rows to 10cm (*3.9in*) over st st worked on No.10 needles

Materials
7 x 25grm balls Templeton's Nylonised 4 ply
One pair No.10 needles
One pair No.12 needles

One No.3.00 (ISR) crochet hook
30cm (*12in*) zip fastener

Left leg
Using No.12 needles cast on 53 sts.
1st row K1, *P1, K1, rep from * to end.
2nd row P1, *K1, P1, rep from * to end.
Rep these 2 rows until work measures 5cm (*2in*) from beg, ending with a 2nd row. Change to No.10 needles. Beg with a K row, cont in st st, inc one st at each end of first and every foll 6th row until there are 73 sts. Cont without shaping until work measures 21cm (*8¼in*) from beg, ending with a P row. **.**
Shape crutch
Dec one st at each end of next and foll alt row, then at end only of foll alt row, ending

with a P row. Leave rem 68 sts on holder. Break off yarn.

Right leg
Work as given for left leg to **.
Shape crutch
Dec one st at each end of next and foll alt row, then at beg only of foll alt row, ending with a P row. 68 sts.
Join legs
Next row K to last st, K next st tog with first st of left leg, K to end. 135 sts.

Above left : Snug, knitted one-piece suit for babies between 6 months and a year.
Right : For the same age group, an easy-to-wear set consisting of jersey, pants and socks.

Cont in st st until work measures 12cm *(4¾in)* from join, ending with a P row.
Next row K1, P7, K119, P7, K1.
Next row K8, P119, K8.
Rep last 2 rows 4 times more.
Next row K1, P7, K7, P105, K7, P7, K1.
Next row K8, P7, K105, P7, K8.
Rep last 2 rows 4 times more.
Next row K1, P7, K7, P7, K91, P7, K7, P7, K1.
Next row K8, P7, K7, P91, K7, P7, K8.
Rep last 2 rows until work measures 46cm *(18in)* from beg, ending with a WS row.
Divide for armholes
Next row Patt 31, cast off 5, patt 63, cast off 5, patt 31.
Cont on last 31 sts for left front. Patt 1 row. Cast off 2 sts at beg of next and foll alt row. Dec one st at beg of foll 2 alt rows. 25 sts. Cont in patt without shaping until armhole measures 8cm *(3¼in)* from beg, ending at armhole edge.
Shape neck
Next row Patt 21, turn and leave rem 4 sts on holder.
Cast off 2 sts at beg of next and foll alt row. Dec one st at beg of foll 3 alt rows. 14 sts. Cont without shaping until armhole measures 12cm *(4¾in)* from beg, ending at armhole edge.

Shape shoulder
Cast off at beg of next and foll alt rows 5 sts twice and 4 sts once.
With WS of work facing, rejoin yarn to back sts and P to end. Cast off 2 sts at beg of next 4 rows. Dec one st at each end of next and foll alt row. 51 sts. Cont without shaping until armholes measure same as left front to shoulder, ending with a P row.
Shape shoulders
Cast off at beg of next and every row 5 sts 4 times and 4 sts twice. Leave rem 23 sts on holder.
With WS of work facing, rejoin yarn to right front sts and complete to match left front, reversing shaping.

Sleeves
Using No.12 needles cast on 41 sts. Work 5cm *(2in)* rib as given for legs, ending with a 2nd row. Change to No.10 needles. Beg with a K row, cont in st st, inc one st at each end of first and every foll 5th row until there are 61 sts. Cont without shaping until sleeve measures 19cm *(7½in)* from beg, ending with a P row.
Shape top
Cast off at beg of next and every row 3 sts twice, one st 10 times, 2 sts 14 times, 3 sts twice and 11 sts once.

Neckband
Join shoulder seams. Using No.12 needles and with RS of work facing, K across sts of right front neck on holder, K up 18 sts up right front neck, K across back neck sts on holder, K up 18 sts down left front neck and K across left front neck sts on holder. 67 sts. Beg with a 2nd row, work 5cm *(2in)* rib as given for legs. Cast off loosely in rib.

6

To make up
Press under a damp cloth with a warm iron. Join sleeve seams. Set in sleeves. Join leg seams. Fold neckband in half to WS and sl st in position. Join front seam for approx 6cm *(2¼in)* from lower edge. Using No.3.00 (ISR) hook and with RS of work facing, work a row of dc down left front and up right front, turn and work a second row. Sew in zip. Press seams.

Jersey, pants & socks set

Sizes
To fit 46[51]cm *(18[20]in)* chest
Jersey length to shoulder, 27[30]cm *(10¾[11¾]in)*
Sleeve seam, 18[20]cm *(7[7¾]in)*
Pants side seam, 18[20]cm *(7[7¾]in)*
The figures in brackets [ ] refer to the 51cm *(20in)* size only
Tension
28 sts and 36 rows to 10cm *(3.9in)* over st st worked on No.10 needles
Materials
Templeton's Nylonised 4 ply
Jersey 4[5] x 25grm balls in main shade, A
1[1] ball of contrast colour, B
1[1] ball of contrast colour, C
Pants 2[3] x 25grm balls in main shade, A
1[1] ball of contrast colour, B
1[1] ball of contrast colour, C
Socks 1[2] x 25grm balls in main shade, A
Oddments of contrast colours, B and C
One pair No.10 needles
One pair No.12 needles
Set of 4 No.10 needles pointed at both ends
Set of 4 No.12 needles pointed at both ends
Waist length of elastic for pants
Narrow elastic for top of socks

Jersey back
Using No.12 needles and A, cast on 67[75] sts.
1st row K1, *P1, K1, rep from * to end.
2nd row P1, *K1, P1, rep from * to end.
Rep these 2 rows until work measures 3cm *(1¼in)* from beg, ending with a 2nd row. Change to No.10 needles. Beg with a K row, cont in st st until work measures 16[18]cm *(6¼[7]in)* from beg, ending with a P row.
Shape raglan
Next row K1, K2 tog, K to last 3 sts, sl 1, K1, psso, K1.
Next row P to end. **
Rep last 2 rows until 29[33] sts rem, ending with a P row. Leave rem sts on holder.

Front
Work as given for back until 43[49] sts rem, ending with a P row.
Shape neck
Next row K1, K2 tog, K15[17], turn and leave rem sts on holder.

Complete this side first. Cast off at beg (neck edge) of next and foll alt rows 3 sts once, 2 sts once and one st 3[4] times, *at the same time* cont to dec one st at raglan edge on every alt row as before until 3 sts rem. Cast off.
With RS of work facing, sl first 7[9] sts on holder for front neck, rejoin yarn to next st, K to last 3 sts, sl 1, K1, psso, K1, P 1 row.
Complete to match first side.

Sleeves
Using No.12 needles and A, cast on 41[43] sts. Work 5cm *(2in)* rib as given for back, ending with a 2nd row. Change to No.10 needles. Beg with a K row, cont in st st and stripe sequence of 4 rows B, 2 rows A, 2 rows C and 6 rows A throughout, inc one st each end of 3rd and every foll 6th row until there are 57[61] sts. Cont without shaping until sleeve measures 18[20]cm *(7[7¾]in)* from beg, ending with a P row.
Shape raglan
Keeping stripe sequence correct, rep from ** to ** as given for back armhole shaping until 19 sts rem, ending with a P row. Leave rem sts on holder.

Neckband
Join raglan seams. Using set of 4 No.12 needles, A and with RS of work facing, K across sts of back neck and left sleeve, K2 tog at seam, K up 13[14] sts down left front neck, K across front neck sts, K up 13[14] sts up right front neck, then K across sts of right sleeve, K last st of sleeve tog with first st of back neck. 98[106] sts. Cont in rounds of K1, P1 rib until neckband measures 5cm *(2in)* from beg. Cast off in rib.

To make up
Press under a damp cloth with a warm iron. Join side and sleeve seams. Fold neckband in half to WS and sl st in position. Press seams.

Pants back
Using No.12 needles and A, cast on 65[73] sts and beg at waist. Work 4cm *(1½in)* rib as given for jersey back, ending with a 2nd row. Change to No.10 needles. Beg with a K row, cont in st st and stripe sequence as given for jersey sleeves until work measures 18[20]cm *(7[7¾]in)* from beg, ending with a P row.
Shape legs
Cast off at beg of next and every row 5 sts twice and 3 sts 14[16] times. 13[15] sts.
**. Cont without shaping for a further 2cm *(¾in)*. Leave rem sts on holder.

Front
Work as given for back to **. Cont without shaping for a further 6cm *(2¼in)*. Leave rem sts on holder.

To make up
Press as given for jersey. Graft sts at crutch. Join side seams.
Leg borders Using set of 4 No.12 needles,

A and with RS of work facing, K up 80[86] sts evenly round legs. Work 5cm (2in) in rounds of K1, P1 rib. Cast off loosely in rib.
Fold borders in half to WS and sl st in position. Insert elastic. Press seams.

Socks

Using set of 4 No.12 needles and A, cast on 44[50] sts. Work 3cm (1¼in) in rounds of K1, P1 rib. Change to set of 4 No.10 needles. Cont in rounds of st st, working in stripe sequence of 4 rounds B, 2 rounds A and 2 rounds C. Break off B and C. Cont in A throughout. Work 2 rounds.

Shape leg

Next round K2 tog, K to last 2 sts, sl 1, K1, psso.
Cont to dec in this way on every foll 5th round until 34[38] sts rem. Cont without shaping until work measures 15[17]cm (6[6¾]in) from beg.

Divide for heel

Next row K9[10], turn and P18[20], then leave rem 16[18] sts on holder for instep.
Work 12[14] rows st st on heel sts, ending with a P row.

Turn heel

1st row K11, sl 1, K1, psso, K1, turn.
2nd row Sl 1, P5[3], P2 tog, P1, turn.
3rd row Sl 1, P6[4], sl 1, K1, psso, K1, turn.
4th row Sl 1, P7[5], P2 tog, P1, turn.
Cont in this way, working one more st on every row, until all sts are worked, ending with a P row. 12 sts. Sl instep sts back on to a needle.
Next round K6; using another needle K6, then K up 8[10] sts along side of heel; using next needle K across instep sts; using 3rd needle K up 8[10] sts along other side of heel, then K6. 44[50] sts.
Next round K to end.
Next round 1st needle K to last 2 sts, K2 tog; 2nd needle K to end; 3rd needle sl 1, K1, psso, K to end.
Rep last 2 rounds 3[4] times more. 36[40] sts. Cont without shaping until work measures 7.5[9]cm (3[3½]in) from back of heel.

Shape toe

Next round *Sl 1, K1, psso, K4[3], rep from * to end. 30[32] sts.
K 1[2] rounds.
Next round *Sl 1, K1, psso, K3[2], rep from * to end. 24 sts.
K 1[2] rounds.
Next round *Sl 1, K1, psso, K2[1], rep from * to end. 18[16] sts.
K 1[2] rounds.
Next round *Sl 1, K1, psso, K1[0], rep from * to end. 12[8] sts.

1st size only

K 1 round.
Next round *Sl 1, K1, psso, rep from * to end. 6 sts.

Both sizes

Break off yarn, thread through rem sts, draw up and fasten off. Fold ribbing at top in half to WS and sl st in position. Insert elastic.

Simple stocking stitch jersey

Sizes

To fit 45.5[51:57]cm (18[20:22]in) chest
Length to shoulder, 27[30:33]cm (10¾[11¾:13]in)
Sleeve seam, 16[18:20]cm (6¼[7:7¾]in)
The figures in brackets [ ] refer to the 51 (20) and 57cm (22in) sizes reseptively

Tension

22 sts and 30 rows to 10cm (3.9in) over st st worked on No.8 needles

Materials

6[6:7] x 25grm balls Lister Superwash Double Knitting
One pair No.8 needles
One pair No.10 needles
10cm (4in) zip fastener

Back

Using No.10 needles cast on 51[57:63] sts.
1st row K1, *P1, K1, rep from * to end.

2nd row P1, *K1, P1, rep from * to end.
Rep last 2 rows until work measures 3cm (1¼in) from beg, ending with a 2nd row and inc one st in centre of last row.
52[58:64] sts. Change to No.8 needles.
Beg with a K row, cont in st st until work measures 16[18:20]cm (6¼[7:7¾]in) from beg, ending with a P row.

Shape armholes

Cast off 3 sts at beg of next 2 rows. Dec one st at each end of next and foll 1[2:3] alt rows. 42[46:50] sts. **. Cont without shaping until armholes measure 3[4:5]cm (1¼[1½:2]in) from beg, ending with a P row.

Divide for opening

Next row K21[23:25], turn and leave rem sts on holder.
Complete this side first.
Next row K2, P to end.

A warm, comfortable jersey is a basic essential of every small child's wardrobe, and this simple stocking stitch jersey with a zip fastener at the back would certainly fit the bill.

Keeping 2 sts at inside edge in g st, cont without shaping until armhole measures 11[12:13]cm *(4¼[4¾ :5]in)* from beg, ending at armhole edge.

Shape shoulder
Cast off at beg of next and foll alt rows 3[3:4] sts twice and 3[4:3] sts once. Leave rem 12[13:14] sts on holder.
With RS of work facing, rejoin yarn to rem sts and K to end.
Next row P to last 2 sts, K2.
Complete to match first side.

Front
Work as given for back to **. Cont without shaping until armholes measure 6[7:8]cm *(2¼[2¾ :3¼]in)* from beg, ending with a P row.

Shape neck
Next row K18[19:20], turn and leave rem sts on holder.
Complete this side first. Cast off 3 sts at beg of next row and 2 sts at beg of foll alt row. Dec one st at neck edge on next and foll 3 alt rows. 9[10:11] sts. Cont without shaping until armhole measures same as back to shoulder, ending at armhole edge.

Shape shoulder
Cast off at beg of next and foll alt rows 3[3:4] sts twice and 3[4:3] sts once.
With RS of work facing, sl first 6[8:10] sts on to holder for centre front neck, rejoin yarn to rem sts and K to end. P 1 row, then complete to match first side.

Sleeves
Using No.10 needles cast on 35[37:39] sts. Work 5cm *(2in)* rib as given for back, ending with a 2nd row. Change to No.8 needles. Beg with a K row, cont in st st, inc one st at each end of 3rd and every foll 6th row until there are 43[47:51] sts. Cont without shaping until sleeve measures 16[18:20]cm *(6¼[7 :7¾]in)* from beg, ending a P row.

Shape top
Cast off 3 sts at beg of next 2 rows. Dec one st at each end of next and foll 7[9:11] alt rows, ending with a P row. Cast off 2 sts at beg of next 6 rows. Cast off rem 9 sts.

Neckband
Join shoulder seams. Using No.10 needles and with RS of work facing, rejoin yarn and K across sts of left back neck on holder, K up 13 sts down left front neck, K across front neck sts on holder, K up 14 sts up right front neck and K across sts of right back neck on holder. 57[61:65] sts.
Next row K2, *P1, K1, rep from * to last st, K1.
Next row K3, *P1, K1, rep from * to last 2 sts, K2.
Rep these 2 rows until neckband measures 5cm *(2in)* from beg. Cast off loosely in rib.

To make up
Press under a damp cloth with a warm iron. Set in sleeves. Join side and sleeve seams. Fold neck band in half to WS and sl st in position. Sew in zip. Press seams.

Striped jersey & pants

Sizes
To fit 46[51]cm *(18[20]in)* chest
Jersey length to shoulder, 27[30]cm *(10¾[11¾]in)*
Sleeve seam, 18[20]cm *(7[7¾]in)*
Pants side seam, 14[16]cm *(5½[6¼]in)*
The figures in brackets [ ] refer to the 51cm *(20in)* size only

Tension
28 sts and 36 rows to 10cm *(3.9in)* over st st worked on No.10 needles

Materials
6[7] x 20grm balls Wendy Peter Pan Darling 4 ply in main shade, A
1 ball of contrast colour, B
One pair No.10 needles
One pair No.12 needles
Set of 4 No.12 needles pointed at both ends

Jersey back
Using No. 12 needles and A, cast on 69[77] sts.
1st row (RS) K1, *P1, K1, rep from * to end.
2nd row P1, *K1, P1, rep from * to end.
Rep these 2 rows until work measures 3cm *(1¼in)* from beg, ending with a 2nd row. Change to No.10 needles. Join in B. Commence patt.
1st row Using B, K2, *sl 1, K3, rep from * to last 3 sts, sl 1, K2.
2nd row Using B, K2, *yfwd, sl 1, ybk, K3, rep from * to last 3 sts, yfwd, sl 1, ybk, K2.
3rd – 4th rows As 1st – 2nd. Break off B.
5th – 14th rows Using A, work in rib as before.
These 14 rows form patt and are rep throughout. Cont in patt until work measures 15[17]cm *(6[6¾]in)* from beg, ending with a WS row.

Shape armhole
Cast off 2[3] sts at beg of next 2 rows. Dec one st at each end of next and foll 3[4] alt rows. 57[61] sts. Cont without shaping until armholes measure 12[13]cm *(4¾[5]in)* from beg, ending with a WS row.

Shape shoulders
Cast off at beg of next and every row 4 sts 4 times and 3[4] sts 4 times. Leave rem 29 sts on holder for back neck.

Front
Work as given for back until armholes measure 7[8]cm *(2¾[3¼]in)* from beg, ending with a WS row.

Shape neck
Next row Patt 22[24] sts, turn and leave rem sts on holder.
Complete this side first. Cast off 3 sts at beg of next row and 2 sts at beg of foll alt row. Keeping armhole edge straight, dec one st at neck edge on next and every foll alt row until 14[16] sts rem. Cont without shaping until front matches back to

shoulder, ending at armhole edge.
Shape shoulder
Cast off at beg of next and foll alt rows 4 sts twice and 3[4] sts twice.
With RS of work facing, sl first 13 sts on to holder for front neck, rejoin yarn to rem sts and patt to end. Patt 1 row. Complete to match first side.

Sleeves
Using No.12 needles and A, cast on 41[45] sts. Work 3cm *(1¼in)* rib as given for back, ending with a 2nd row. Change to No.10 needles. Join in B. Cont in patt as given for back, inc one st at each end of 5th and every foll 6th row until there are 61[65] sts. Cont without shaping until sleeve measures approx 18[20]cm *(7[7¾]in)* from beg, ending with same patt row as back at underarm.

Shape top
Cast off at beg of next and every row 2 sts twice, one st 10[14] times, 2 sts 18 times and 11 sts once.

Neckband
Join shoulder seams. Using set of 4 No.12 needles, A and with RS of work facing, rib across back neck sts on holder, K up 21 sts down left front neck, rib across front neck sts on holder and K up 21 sts up right front neck. 84 sts. Work in rounds of rib until neckband measures 5cm *(2in)* from beg. Cast off loosely in rib.

To make up
Do not press. Set in sleeves. Join side and sleeve seams. Fold neckband in half to WS and sl st in position.

Pants back
Using No.10 needles and A, cast on 23 sts. Work 7cm *(2¾in)* rib as given for jersey.
**Shape legs
Cont in rib, cast on at beg of next and every row one st 4[6] times, 2 sts 12[14] times and 10[11] sts twice. 71[79] sts. Mark each end of last row. Cont without shaping until work measures 14[16] cm *(5½[6¼]in)* from markers, ending with a WS row.
Next row (eyelet hole row) K1, *yfwd, K2 tog, rep from * to end.
Rib 4 more rows. Cast off loosely in rib.

Front
Using No.10 needles and A, cast on 23 sts. Work 4cm *(1½in)* rib as given for jersey back. Cont as given for pants back from ** to end.

To make up
Do not press. Join side and crutch seams. Turn 1cm *(½in)* hem round legs to WS and sl st in position. Using 4 strands of yarn, make a twisted cord approx 80cm *(32in)* long and thread through eyelet holes. Knot each end of cord and tease out ends into tassels.

Right : Jersey with woven-look stripes and pants with drawstring waist.

Crochet dungarees with motif

Sizes

To fit 51[56:61]cm *(20[22:24]in)* chest
Length of inside leg, 31.5[36:40]cm
(12½[14¼:15¾]in)
The figures in brackets [ ] refer to the 56
(22) and 61cm *(24in)* sizes respectively

Tension

21 sts and 15 rows to 10cm *(3.9in)* over htr
worked on No.3.50 (ISR) crochet hook

Materials

10[11:12] x 25grm balls of Jaeger Sheridan
Crepe 4 ply in main shade, A
Oddments of 3 contrast colours, B, C and
D for motif
One No.3.50 (ISR) crochet hook
One No.3.00 (ISR) crochet hook
2 buttons

Left leg

Using No.3.50 (ISR) hook and A, make
64[69:74]ch.

*Above left : Neat crochet dungarees for a
little boy or girl, with contrast circular motif
on the bib. Right : Baby's crochet dress with
frilled sleeves and hemline.*

1st row Into 3rd ch from hook work 1htr,
1htr into each ch to end. Turn. 63[68:73]
htr.
2nd row 2ch to count as first htr, miss
first htr, 1htr into each htr to end. Turn.
Cont in htr until work measures
14[17:20]cm *(5½[6¾:7¾]in)* from beg. Inc
one st at each end of next and every foll 3rd
row until there are 79[84:89] sts. Cont
without shaping until work measures
31.5[36:40]cm *(12½[14¼:15¾]in)* from beg.

Shape crutch
Next row Ss over first 2 sts, patt to last 2 sts, turn.
Rep last row 3 times more. Work 3 rows without shaping, then dec one st at each end of next and foll 4th row. 59[64:69] sts. Break off yarn and leave for time being. Work right leg to match. Do not break off yarn.
Join legs
Next row Patt across sts of right leg to last st, work last st tog with first st of left leg, patt to end. Turn. 117[127:137] sts.
Cont without shaping until work measures 24[26:28]cm (9½[10¼:11]in) from beg of crutch shaping. Break off yarn and turn. Miss first 28[31:34] sts, rejoin yarn to next st, 2ch, patt to last 28[31:34] sts, turn, 61[65:69] sts.
Next row Ss over first 6 sts, patt to last 6 sts, turn.
Next row Ss over first 4[5:6] sts, patt to last 4[5:6] sts, turn.
Dec 2 sts at each end of next and foll alt row, then work 1 row. 33[35:37] sts.
Next row 2 ch, work 6htr, turn.
Cont on these 7 sts for 21[23:25]cm (8¼[9:9¾]in) or required length of strap. Fasten off.
Return to where work was left, miss next 19[21:23] sts, rejoin yarn to next st, 2ch, patt to end. Complete to match first strap.

Motif
Using No.3.00 (ISR) hook and B, make 4ch. Join with a ss to first ch to form circle.
1st round 5ch to count as first dtr and 1ch, *1dtr into circle, 1ch, rep from * 10 times more. Join with a ss to 4th of first 5ch.
2nd round Ss into first 1ch sp, 4ch to count as first tr and 1ch, 1tr into same sp, *(1tr, 1ch, 1tr) into next sp, rep from * 10 times more. Join with a ss to 3rd of first 4ch. Break off B.
3rd round Join in C to any 1ch sp, 5ch to count as first tr and 2ch, 1tr into same sp, *1ch, (1tr, 2ch, 1tr) into next sp, rep from * 10 times more, 1ch. Join with a ss to 3rd of first 5ch.
4th round Using C, ss into first 2ch sp, 3ch to count as first tr, 3tr into same sp, *1ch, 4tr into next 2ch sp, rep from * 10 times more, 1ch. Join with a ss to 3rd of first 3ch. Break off C.
5th round Join in B to any 1ch sp, 4ch to count as first tr and 1ch, 1tr into same sp, *(1tr, 1ch, 1tr) between 2nd and 3rd of 4tr, (1tr, 1ch, 1tr) into next 1ch sp, rep from * 10 times more, (1tr, 1ch, 1tr) between 2nd and 3rd of 4tr. Join with a ss to 3rd of first 4ch. Break off B.
6th round Join in D to any 1ch sp and work as 3rd round. Fasten off.

To make up
Press lightly under a damp cloth with a warm iron. Join leg seams. Join back seam and crutch shaping on front.
Edging Using No.3.50 (ISR) hook, A and with RS of work facing, work a row of dc right round top edge, making a button loop at each end of strap. Turn and work a 2nd row of dc, working in dc round button loops. Fasten off.
Press seams. Sew on buttons. Sew on motif to front.

Baby's dress with frills

Sizes
To fit 45.5[51:56]cm (18[20:22]in) chest
Length to shoulder 31.5[36:40]cm (12½[14¼:15¾]in)
Sleeve seam, 4cm (1½in)
The figures in brackets [ ] refer to the 51 (20) and 56cm (22in) sizes respectively
Tension
22 sts and 18 rows to 10cm (3.9in) over patt worked on No.3.00 (ISR) crochet hook
Materials
5[5:6] x 20grm balls of Sirdar Wash 'n' Wear 4 ply in main shade, A
1 ball of contrast colour, B
One No.3.00 (ISR) crochet hook

Back
Using No.3.00 (ISR) hook and A, make 94[104:114]ch.
1st row (RS) Into 4th ch from hook work 1tr, 1tr into each ch to end. Turn. 92[102:112]tr.
2nd row 1ch to count as first dc, miss first tr, 1dc into each dc to end. Turn.
3rd row 3ch to count as first tr, miss first dc, 1tr into each dc to end. Turn.
The 2nd and 3rd rows form the patt and are rep throughout. Work 1 row patt.
Shape skirt
5th row 3ch, work 2tr, 2tr tog, work 26[30:34]tr, 2tr tog, work 26[28:30]tr, 2tr tog, work 26[30:34]tr, 2tr tog, work 3tr. Turn.
Work 3 rows patt without shaping.
9th row 3ch, work 2tr, 2tr tog, work 24[28:32]tr, 2tr tog, work 26[28:30]tr, 2tr tog, work 24[28:32]tr, 2tr tog, work 3tr. Turn.
Work 3 rows patt without shaping. Cont to dec in this way on next and every foll 4th row until 56[62:68] sts rem. Cont without shaping until work measures 21[24:27]cm (8¼[9½:10¾]in) from beg, ending with a WS row.
Shape armholes
Next row Ss over first 3dc, 3ch, patt to last 3dc, turn.
Next row Patt to end.
Next row Ss over first 2dc, 3ch, patt to last 2dc, turn.
Next row Patt to end.
Next row 3ch, 2tr tog, patt to last 3dc, 2tr tog, 1tr. Turn.
Rep last 2 rows 1[2:3] times more. 42[46:50] sts. Cont without shaping until armholes measure 11[11.5:12.5]cm (4¼[4¾:5]in) from beg, ending with a WS row.
Shape shoulders
Dec 4 sts at each end of next 2 rows, then 3[4:5] sts at each end of next row. 20[22:24] sts. Fasten off.

Front
Work as given for back until armholes measure 6[7:8]cm (2¼[2¾:3¼]in) from beg, ending with a WS row.
Shape neck
Next row Patt over first 11[12:13] sts, turn.
Cont on these sts until armhole measures same as back to shoulder, ending at armhole edge.
Shape shoulder
Next row Ss over first 4 sts, patt to end. Turn.
Next row Patt to last 4 sts, turn. Fasten off.
Return to where work was left, miss first 20[22:24] sts for centre front neck, rejoin yarn to next st and patt to end. Complete to match first side, reversing shaping.

Sleeves
Using No.3.00 (ISR) hook and A, make 35[38:41]ch. Work first 2 rows as given for back. 33[36:39] sts. Cont in patt as given for back, inc one st at each end of next and foll 2 alt rows, then work 1 row. 39[42:45] sts.
Shape top
Next row Ss over first 4 sts, patt to last 4 sts, turn.
Dec one st at each end of next 5[6:7] rows, then 2 sts at each end of next 2 rows, then 3 sts at each end of next row. 7[8:9] sts. Fasten off.
Frills
Using No.3.00 (ISR) hook, A and with RS of work facing, rejoin yarn to beg of commencing ch of sleeve and work along lower edge as foll:
Next row 3ch, miss 2ch, *(1tr, 3ch, 1tr) into next ch, miss 2ch, rep from * to last ch, 1tr into last ch. Fasten off.
Using No.3.00 (ISR) hook, B and with RS of work facing, rejoin yarn to top of first 3ch, 1ch, 1dc into each st to end. Fasten off.
Work frills in same way along every 4th row of sleeves, noting that this is the dc row. To work these, fold the work along the row to be worked, then with the top of the sleeve towards you, work into the dc of the row.

To make up
Do not press. Join shoulder seams. Set in sleeves. Join side and sleeve seams. Work frill rows along lower edge of skirt, then work a second row on the 4th row up from lower edge. Using No.3.00 (ISR) hook, A and with RS of work facing, work a row of dc round neck edge, then a row of crab st with B, working in dc from left to right instead of from right to left. Fasten off. Press seams under a dry cloth with a cool iron.

11

Angel top pants & bootees

Sizes
To fit 51cm *(20in)* chest
Angel top length, 28cm *(11in)*
Sleeve seam, 16cm *(6¼in)*
Pants length at centre front, 22cm *(8¾in)*

Tension
26 sts and 38 rows to 10cm *(3.9in)* over st
st worked on No.10 needles; 29 sts and 40
rows to 10cm *(3.9in)* over patt worked on
No.10 needles

Materials
5 x 20grm balls Sunbeam Baby QuickKnit
in main shade, A
4 balls of contrast colour, B
One pair No.10 needles
One No.10 circular Twin-Pin
One No.3.00 (ISR) crochet hook
Cable needle
Waist length of elastic

Angel top back
Using No.10 needles and B, cast on 74 sts.

*Loose, lacy angel top with pompon cords
plus matching pants and bootees.*

K 13 rows g st.
Next row P5, *P twice into next st, P8, rep from * 6 times more, P twice into next st, P5. 82 sts.
Break off B. Join in A. Commence patt.
1st row (RS) K2, *yfwd, sl next st on to cable needle and hold at back of work, K2 tog, then K1 from cable needle, sl next 2 sts on to cable needle and hold at front of work, K1, then K2 tog tbl from cable needle, yfwd, K3, rep from * to end, finishing with K2 instead of K3.
2nd row P to end.
3rd row P2, *K6, P3, rep from * to last 8 sts, K6, P2.
4th row K2, *P6, K3, rep from * to last 8 sts, P6, K2.
Rep last 4 rows until work measures 16cm (6¼in) from beg, ending with a WS row.

Shape armholes
Keeping patt correct, cast off 2 sts at beg of next 4 rows. Dec one st at each end of next and foll 4 alt rows, ending with a WS row. 64 sts. Break off yarn. Leave sts on holder.

Angel top front
Work as given for back.

Sleeves
Using No.10 needles and B, cast on 50 sts. K 13 rows g st.
Next row P6, *P twice into next st, P8, rep from * 3 times more, P twice into next st, P7. 55 sts.
Break off B. Join in A. Cont in patt as given for back until work measures 16cm (6¼in) from beg, ending with same patt row as back to underarm.
Shape top
Rep from ** to ** as given for back armhole shaping. 37 sts. Break off yarn. Leave sts on holder.

Yoke
Using No.10 circular Twin-Pin, B and with RS of work facing, K across sts of back, left sleeve, front and right sleeve, K2 tog at each seam. 198 sts. Work 5 rounds g st (1st round P, 2nd round K). Join in A. Work 7 rounds st st (every round K).
Next round K2, *K2 tog, K4, rep from * to last 4 sts, K2 tog, K2. 165 sts.
Using B and beg with a K round, work 6 rounds g st.
Next round Using A, K1, *K2 tog, K3, rep from * to last 4 sts, K2 tog, K2. 132 sts.
Using A, work 6 rounds st st.
Next round Using A, K5, *K2 tog, K9, rep from * to last 6 sts, K2 tog, K4. 120 sts.
Next round Using B, *K2 tog, yfwd, rep * to last 2 sts, K2 tog. 119 sts.
Using B and beg with a P round, work 4 rounds g st.
Cast off loosely P-wise.

To make up
Do not press. Join raglan, then side and sleeve seams. Make a twisted cord in B, about 80cm (31½in) long, and thread

through holes at neck. Decorate each end of cord with a pom-pon.

Pants front
Using No.10 needles and B, cast on 14 sts for crutch. Beg with a K row, work 6 rows st st. Cast on at beg of next and every row 2 sts 28 times. 70 sts. Cont without shaping until work measures 20cm (7¾in) from beg, ending with a K row. K 8 rows g st. Cast off.

Pants back
Using No.10 needles and B, cast on 14 sts. Beg with a K row, cont in st st, inc one st at each end of 2nd and foll 5 alt rows. 26 sts. Cast on at beg of next and every row 2 sts 22 times. 70 sts. Cont without shaping until work measures 20cm (7¾in) from beg, ending with a P row.
Shape back
Next row K to last 7 sts, turn.
Next row P to last 7 sts, turn.
Next row K to last 14 sts, turn.
Cont working 7 sts less on every row 5 times more.
Next row K to end.
K 8 rows g st. Cast off.

To make up
Do not press. Join side seams.
Leg border Using No.10 needles, B and with RS of work facing, K up 82 sts evenly round legs. K 16 rows g st. Cast off loosely. Fold leg borders in half to WS and sl st in position. Join crutch seam. Work herringbone casing over elastic on WS of waist.

Bootees
Using No.10 needles and A, cast on 42 sts. K 18 rows g st.
Next row K2, *yfwd, K2 tog, K2, rep from * to end.
Next row K to end.
Divide for instep
Do not break off yarn, but sl first 15 sts on to a holder, join in B and K12, turn. K 19 rows g st on these 12 sts for instep. Break off B.
Sl 15 sts from holder back on to needle, with RS of work facing and using A, K15, K up 11 sts along side of instep, K12 instep sts, K up 11 sts along other side of instep, K15. 64 sts. K 11 rows g st. Break off yarn.
Shape foot
Sl first 26 sts on to right hand needle, join in B, K11, K2 tog tbl, turn.
Next row K11, K2 tog tbl, turn.
Rep last row 38 times more. 24 sts. Fold work with back seam in centre of one piece and graft sts tog for heel.

To make up
Join back seam. Using No.3.00 (ISR) hook and B, work 1 round dc, then 1 round crab st (work in dc from left to right) around top edge. Work around outer edge of sole in dc. Make twisted cords in B, about 60cm (23½in) long, and thread through holes at ankle.

Cardigan with bonnet

Sizes
To fit 46-51cm (18-20in) chest
Length to shoulder, 27cm (10¾in)
Sleeve seam, 15cm (6in)
Tension
23 sts and 16 rows to 10cm (3.9in) over patt worked on No.3.00 (ISR) crochet hook
Materials
4 x 25grm balls Hayfield Beaulon 4 ply in main shade, A
2 balls of contrast colour, B
1 ball of contrast colour, C
One No.3.00 (ISR) crochet hook
3 buttons

Jacket back and fronts
Using No.3.00 (ISR) hook and A, make 129ch and work in one piece to underarm.
1st row (WS) Into 3rd ch from hook work 1dc, 1dc into each ch to end. Turn. 128 sts.
2nd row 3ch to count as first tr, miss first dc, 1tr into each dc, ending with last tr into turning ch. Turn.
3rd row 1ch to count as first dc, 1dc into each tr, ending with last dc into 3rd of 3ch. Turn.
4th row As 2nd row, joining in B on last tr.
5th row Using B, as 3rd row.
6th row Using B, 3ch, *miss 2dc, 1dtr into next dc, 1tr into each of 2 missed dc, working behind dtr – called crossed tr group –, rep from * to end, 1tr into turning ch. Turn.
7th row Using B, 1ch, 1dc into each st to end. Turn.
8th row As 6th, joining in A on last tr.
9th row Using A, as 7th row.
10th row 3ch, 1tr into each of next 33dc, work 2tr tog, 1tr into each of next 56dc, work 2tr tog, 1tr into each of next 33dc, 1tr into turning ch. Turn. 126 sts.
11th row As 3rd row.
12th row 3ch, 1tr into each of next 33dc, work 2tr tog, 1tr into each of next 54dc, work 2tr tog, 1tr into each of next 33dc, 1tr into turning ch, joining in B on last tr. 124 sts.
13th row As 5th row.
14th row 3ch, work 11 crossed tr groups over next 33 sts, 1tr into next st, work 18 crossed tr groups over next 54 sts, 1tr into next st, work 11 crossed tr groups over next 33 sts, 1tr into turning ch. Turn.
15th row 1ch, 1dc into each of next 33 sts, miss 1tr, 1dc into each of next 54 sts, miss 1tr, 1dc into each of next 33 sts, 1dc into 3rd of 3ch. Turn. 122 sts.
16th row As 6th row, joining in A on last tr. Turn.
Rep 9th row, then 2nd-8th rows again.
Divide for armholes
1st row Using A, 1ch, 1dc into each of next 26 sts, work 2dc tog, turn.
Cont on these sts for left front. Patt 4 rows, dec one st at armhole edge on every row.

13

A useful cardigan for extra warmth, crocheted in three colours, with a snug bonnet made up to match the cardigan yoke.

24 sts.

6th row Dec 1, patt to last 10 sts, turn. 13 sts.

7th row Ss over first 4 sts, patt to last 2 sts, dec 1. 8 sts.

8th row Dec 1, patt to last 3 sts, fasten off.
With WS of work facing, miss next 3 sts, rejoin A to next st, 1ch, work 2dc tog, 1dc into each of next 53dc, work 2dc tog, turn. Cont on these 56 sts for back. Patt 7 rows, dec one st at each end of every row. 42 sts.
With WS of work facing, miss next 3 sts, rejoin A to next st, 1ch, work 2dc tog, patt to end. Cont on these 28 sts for right front, working to match left front.

Sleeves

Using No.3.00 (ISR) hook and A, make 36ch. Work 1st-2nd rows as given for back and fronts, joining in B on last tr of 2nd row. 35 sts.

3rd row As 5th row of back and fronts.

4th row As 6th row of back and fronts, joining in A on last tr.
These 4 rows form sleeve patt. Cont in patt, inc one st at each end of next and every foll 4th row until there are 45 sts. Patt 3 more rows.

Shape top
Cont in patt, dec one st at each end of every row until 29 sts rem. Fasten off.

Yoke

Using No.3.00 (ISR) hook, B and with WS of work facing, work 1 row ss across left front, left sleeve, back right sleeve and right front, dec one st at each seam. 138 sts. Break off B.

Next row (RS) Using A, 1ch, work 1dc into each ss, working into back loop of ss and front loop of st on previous row at same time. Break off A. Do not turn.

Next row (RS) Using C, 1ch, work 1dc into each dc, working into back loops of sts on previous row. Turn.

Next row Using C, 3ch, 1tr into front loop only of each dc to end. Turn.

Next row Using C, 1ch, 1dc into back loop only of each tr to end. Turn. Break off C.

Next row Using A, 1ch, 1dc into each dc, working into both loops of sts on previous row. Turn.

Next row 3ch, working into both loops throughout, *1tr into next st, work 2tr tog, rep from * 44 times more, 1tr into each of last 2 sts, turn. 93 sts.
Work 1 row dc, 1 row tr and 1 row dc.

Next row 3ch, *1tr into next st, work 2tr tog, rep from * 29 times more, 1tr into each of last 2 sts. Turn. 63 sts.
Work 1 row dc and 1 row tr.

Next row 1ch, 1dc into each of next 4 sts, work 2dc tog, *1dc into each of next 8 sts, work 2dc tog, rep from * 4 times more, 1dc into each of last 6 sts. Fasten off.

To make up
Do not press. Join raglan and sleeve seams. Using No.3.00 (ISR) hook, A and with RS of work facing, work 1 row dc, then 1 row crab st (work in dc from left to right instead of right to left) all round outer edges. Sew 3 buttons to left front yoke. Make 3 loops on right front yoke to correspond.

Hat
Using No.3.00 (ISR) hook and A, make 85ch. Work 1st row as given for jacket. 84 sts. Rep 2nd and 3rd rows of jacket 8 times.

18th row 3ch, 1tr into next st, work 2tr tog, *1tr into each of next 2 sts, work 2 tr tog, rep from * to end. Turn. 63 sts.

19th row Work in dc. Turn.

20th row 3ch, work 2tr tog, *1tr into next st, work 2tr tog, rep from * to end. Turn. 42 sts.

21st row Work in dc. Turn.

22nd row 3ch, *work 2tr tog, rep from * to last st, 1tr into last st. Turn. 22 sts.

23rd row Work in dc. Turn.

24th row As 22nd. 12 sts.
Break off yarn, thread through rem sts, draw up and fasten off.

Ear flaps
With RS of work facing, miss 10 sts along cast on edge, join in A to next st, 3ch, 1tr into each of next 8 sts, turn.

Next row 1ch, miss 1tr, 1dc into each of next 5tr, miss 1tr, 1dc into 3rd of 3ch. Turn. 7 sts.

Next row 3ch, work 2tr tog, 1tr into next dc, work 2tr tog, 1tr into turning ch. Turn. 5 sts.

Next row 1ch, miss 1tr, 1dc into next tr, miss 1tr, 1dc into 3rd of 3ch. Turn. 3 sts. Fasten off.
Work second ear flap in same way.

To make up
Do not press. Join back seam.

Edging Using No.3.00 (ISR) hook and C, make 6ch, with RS of work facing, ss into middle dc of left ear flap, cont in dc along back of ear flap, hat and right ear flap to centre, 7ch, turn.

Next row 1dc into 3rd ch from hook, 1htr into each of next 2ch, 1tr into each of next 2ch, 1tr into front loop only of each dc to last 6ch, 1tr into each of next 2ch, 1htr into each of next 2ch, 1dc into each of next 2ch. Turn.

Next row 1ch, 1dc into back loop only of each tr to end. Fasten off.
Work in same way round front edges of ear flaps and hat.
Using 5 strands of C make a twisted cord and sew to point of each ear flap.

Shell edged cot blanket

Size
Approx 85cm (33½in) long x 80cm (31½in) wide
Tension
18 sts and 10 rows to 10cm (3.9in) over tr worked on No.3.50 (ISR) crochet hook
Materials
19 x 25grm balls Sunbeam Hyland Superwash DK in main shade, A
1 ball of contrast colour, B
One No.3.50 (ISR) crochet hook

Blanket

Using No.3.50 (ISR) hook and A, make 145ch.
Base row Into 3rd ch from hook work 1dc, 1dc into each ch to end. Turn. 144 sts.
Next row 3ch to count as first tr, 1tr into each st to end. Turn.
Rep last row until work measures 85cm (33½in) from beg. Fasten off.
Edging Using No.3.50 (ISR) hook, join B into top left hand corner and cont working down side edge, 3ch, 7tr into corner st where yarn was joined, *miss 1 row end, 1dc into next row end, miss 1 row end, 5tr into next row end, rep from * along side, work 8tr into corner, cont along lower edge, **miss 2tr, 1dc between tr, miss 3tr, 5tr between tr, rep from ** along lower edge, work 8tr into corner, then cont along other 2 sides as before. Fasten off.
Press under a damp cloth with a warm iron.

Yoked jersey with ducks

Sizes
To fit 45.5cm (18in) chest
Length to shoulder, 30cm (11¾in)
Sleeve seam, 19cm (7½in)
Tension
30 sts and 40 rows to 10cm (3.9in) over st st worked on No.11 needles
Materials
5 x 25grm balls Sunbeam Hyland Superwash Wool 4 ply in main shade, A
Oddments of contrast colours, B and C, for embroidery
One pair No.11 needles
One pair No.12 needles
One No.12 circular Twin-Pin

Back

Using No.12 needles cast on 79 sts.
1st row K1, *P1, K1, rep from * to end.
2nd row P1, *K1, P1, rep from * to end.
Rep last 2 rows until work measures 3cm (1¼in) from beg, ending with a 2nd row and inc one st at end of last row. 80 sts. Change to No.11 needles. Beg with a K row, cont in st st until work measures 18cm (7in) from beg, ending with a P row.
Shape armholes
Next row K2, sl 1, K1, psso, K to last 4 sts, K2 tog, K2.
Next row P to end.
Rep last 2 rows 10 times more. **. 58 sts.
Break off yarn.
Leave sts on holder.

Front
Work as given for back.

Sleeves
Using No.12 needles cast on 45 sts. Work 5cm (2in) rib as given for back, ending with a 2nd row. Change to No.11 needles. Beg with a K row, cont in st st, inc one st at each end of 5th and every foll 4th row, until there are 63 sts. Cont without shaping until sleeve measures 19cm (7½in) from beg, ending with a P row.
Shape top
Rep from ** to ** as given for back armhole shaping. 41 sts. Break off yarn.
Leave sts on holder.

Yoke
Using No.12 circular Twin-Pin and with RS of work facing, beg with back and K across all sts on holders, K2 tog on each piece at each seam. 190 sts. P 1 round, then K 1 round.
Next round *P2, (P2 tog, P4) 9 times across back sts, (P2 tog, P5) 5 times, P2 tog, P2 across sleeve sts, rep from * once more. 160 sts.
Cont in rounds of K1, P1 rib for 4cm (1½in).
Next round *K2, (K2 tog, K3) 9 times across back sts, (K2 tog, K4) 5 times, K2 tog, K1 across sleeve sts, rep from * once more. 130 sts.
P 1 round, K 1 round, then P 1 round.
Work 2 rounds K1, P1 rib.
Next round *K2 tog tbl, yfwd, rep from * to end. Rib 1 more round. Cast off loosely in rib.

To make up
Press under a damp cloth with a warm iron. Join raglan, then side and sleeve seams. Using 4 strands of yarn, make a twisted cord and thread through holes at neck. Embroider ducks in Swiss darning from chart, reversing chart for opposite directions. Press seams.

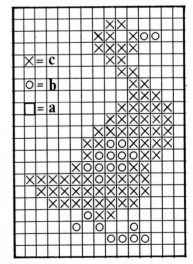

X = c
O = b
☐ = a

Left : Soft crochet cot blanket with attractive shell edging, plus an easy-to-wear baby's jersey with drawstring neck and cheerful embroidered ducks (see chart).

Baby's wide~stripe pullover

Sizes

To fit 41[46:51]cm *(16[18:20]in)* chest

Length to shoulder, 22[24:26]cm
(8¾[9½:10¼]in)
Sleeve seam, 15[17:19]cm *(6[6¾:7½]in)*
The figures in brackets [ ] refer to the 46
(18) and 51cm *(20in)* sizes respectively

Tension

26 sts and 34 rows to 10cm *(3.9in)* over st
st worked on No.10 needles

Materials

2[2:3] x 50grm balls Pingouin Super 4 in
main shade, A

2[2:2] balls of contrast colour, B
One pair No.10 needles
One No.2.50 (ISR) crochet hook
1 button

Front

Using No.10 needles and A, cast on
55[60:65] sts. Beg with a K row, work 20
rows st st. Join in B. Cont in st st and stripe
sequence of 10 rows B and 10 rows A until
work measures 16[18:20]cm *(6¼[6¾:7¾]in)*

16

from beg, ending with a P row.

Shape armholes
Cont in stripe sequence throughout, cast off 6 sts at beg of next 2 rows. 43[48:53] sts. Cont without shaping until work measures 23[25:27]cm *(9[9¾ :10¾]in)* from beg, ending with a P row.

Shape neck
Next row K11[12:13], cast off 21[24:27] sts, K to end.
Cont on last 11[12:13] sts until work

measures 25[27:29]cm *(9¾[10¾ :11½]in)* from beg, ending with a P row. Cast off. With WS of work facing, rejoin yarn to rem sts and complete to match first side.

Right back
Using No.10 needles and A, cast on 45[48:51] sts. Work to match front to underarm, ending with a P row.

Shape armhole
Cast off 6 sts at beg of next row. 39[42:45]

sts. Cont without shaping until work matches front to shoulder, ending with a P row. Cast off.

Left back
Work as given for right back, reversing shaping.

Sleeves
Using No.10 needles and B, cast on 54[56:58] sts. Beg with a K row, work 20 rows st st. Join in A. Cont in st st and stripe sequence of 10 rows A and 10 rows B until work measures 20[22:24]cm *(7¾[8¾ :9½]in)* from beg, ending with a P row. Cast off.

To make up
Do not press. Join shoulder seams. Set in sleeves, sewing last 2cm *(¾in)* of sleeve seam to cast off sts at underarm. Turn 10 rows to WS at lower and sleeve edges for hem and sl st in position. Turn 2cm *(¾in)* to WS down each side of back opening and sl st in position. Using No.2.50 (ISR) hook, same colour as cast off sts at front neck and with RS of work facing, work 1 row dc round neck edge. Lap right back over left, make a button loop at neck edge on right back. Sew on button to correspond.

Two~colour sleeping bag

Sizes
To fit approx 1–3 months [3-6 months]
Length 49[56]cm *(19¼[22]in)*
The figures in brackets [ ] refer to the 3–6 month size only

Tension
25 sts and 46 rows to 10cm *(3.9in)* over ridge patt worked on No.10 needles

Materials
3 x 50grm balls Pingouin Super 4 in main shade, A
Oddment of contrast colour, B
One pair No.10 needles
One pair No.12 needles
One No.2.50 (ISR) crochet hook
2 buttons

Front
Using No.10 needles and A, cast on 79[85] sts. K 5 rows. P 1 row. These 6 rows form ridge patt. Cont in patt, dec one st at each end of 9th and every foll 10th row until 51[57] sts rem. Cont without shaping until work measures approx 32[35]cm *(12½[13¾]in)* from beg, ending with a 6th patt row. Change to No.12 needles.
Next row (RS) K1, *P1, K1, rep from * to end.

Comfortable jersey with straight sleeves for the small baby, teamed with a matching sleeping bag with buttoned straps.

Next row P1, *K1, P1, rep from * to end.
Rep last 2 rows for 5cm *(2in)*, ending with a WS row. **.
Shape armholes
Cont in rib, cast off 10[11] sts at beg of next 2 rows. Cont on rem 31[35] sts until armholes measure 3[4]cm *(1¼[1½]in)* from beg, ending with a WS row.
Next row (buttonhole row) Rib 5, cast off 3, rib to last 8 sts, cast off 3, rib to end.
Next row Rib to end, casting on 3 sts over those cast off in previous row.
Cont in rib for a further 2cm *(¾in)*. Cast off.

Back
Work as given for front to **.
Shape armholes
Cast off 4[5] sts at beg of next 2 rows. Dec one st at each end of next and foll 5 alt rows. 31[35] sts. Cont without shaping until back measures same as front, ending with a WS row.
Divide for straps
Next row Rib 11, cast off 9[13], rib to end. Cont in rib on last 11 sts for 14[16]cm *(5½[6¼]in)*. Cast off.
With WS of work facing, rejoin yarn to rem 11 sts and complete to match.

Base
Using No.10 needles and A, cast on 44[48] sts. Cont in g st, inc one st at each end of every alt row until there are 62[68] sts. K 8 rows without shaping. Dec one st at each end of next and every alt row until 44[48] sts rem.
Cast off.

To make up
Do not press. Join side seams and sew in base. Using No.2.50 (ISR) hook and B, work a row of dc round seam at base. Join with a ss into first dc.
Next round *3ch, miss 1dc, 1dc into next dc, rep from * to end. Fasten off.
Using No.2.50 (ISR) hook, B and with RS of work facing, work a row of dc round all top edges and straps. Fasten off.
Embroidery Using B throughout, work on rib part of bodice in cross stitch on every K rib as shown in picture.
On main section, beg at left hand side, bring needle up below second st on first ridge, insert into 3rd st on 4th ridge, back up through same st as before, into 3rd st on 4th ridge again, out on 7th st on first ridge, *miss 4 sts on 4th ridge, insert needle into next st, out again into same st as before, back into same st on 4th ridge, miss 4 sts on first ridge, bring needle out below next st, rep from * along row.
Beg again at left hand side on 5th ridge and cont in same way, working between stitches in first line.
Using B make a twisted cord approx 40[45]cm *(15¾[17¾]in)* long and thread through alternate K sts at beg of rib. Make 2 pom-pons in B and sew to either side of ribbed section.
Sew a button to end of each strap.

Sun suit with straps

Sizes
To fit 9 to 18 months
Chest approx 51cm *(20in)*
Tension
32 sts and 38 rows to 10cm *(3.9in)* over patt worked on No.11 needles
Materials
4 x 20 grm balls Wendy Peter Pan Darling 4 ply
One pair No.11 needles
One pair No.12 needles
Cable needle
0.45 metres *(½ yard)* narrow elastic
2 buttons

Front
Using No.11 needles cast on 22 sts for crutch.
Shape crutch and legs
1st row (RS) P1, sl 1, K1, psso, K16, K2 tog, P1.
2nd row K1, P18, K1, turn and cast on one st.
3rd row P2, sl 1, K1, psso, K14, K2 tog, P1, turn and cast on one st.
4th row K2, P16, K2, turn and cast on 6 sts.
5th row P2, K4, P2, sl 1, K1, psso, K12, K2 tog, P2, turn and cast on 6 sts.
6th row K2, P4, K2, P14, K2, P4, K2, turn and cast on 4 sts.
7th row P2, K2 tog, yrn, P2, K4, P2, sl 1, K1, psso, K10, K2 tog, P2, K4, P2, turn and cast on 4 sts.
8th row K2, P2, K2, P4, K2, P12, K2, P4, K2, P2, K2, turn and cast on 6sts.
9th row P2, K4, P2, yon, sl 1, K1, psso, P2, sl next 2 sts on to cable needle and hold at front of work, K2, then K2 from cable needle – called C4 –, P2, sl 1, K1, psso, K8, K2 tog, P2, C4, P2, yon, sl 1, K1, psso, P2, turn and cast on 6 sts.
10th row K2, P4, K2, P2, K2, P4, K2, P10, K2, P4, K2, P2, K2, P4, K2, turn and cast on 4 sts.
11th row (P2, K2 tog, yrn, P2, K4) twice, P2, sl 1, K1, psso, K6, K2 tog, P2, K4, P2, K2 tog, yrn, P2, K4, P2, turn and cast on 4 sts.
12th row (K2, P2, K2, P4) twice, K2, P8, K2, (P4, K2, P2, K2) twice, turn and cast on 6 sts.
13th row (P2, K4, P2, yon, sl 1, K1, psso) twice, P2, K4, P2, sl 1, K1, psso, K4, K2 tog, P2, (K4, P2, yon, sl 1, K1, psso, P2) twice, turn and cast on 6 sts.
14th row (K2, P4, K2, P2) twice, K2, P4, K2, P6, K2, P4, K2, (P2, K2, P4, K2) twice, turn and cast on 4 sts.
15th row (P2, K2 tog, yrn, P2, C4) 3 times, P2, sl 1, K1, psso, K2, K2 tog, P2, (C4, P2, K2 tog, yrn, P2) twice, C4, P2, turn and cast on 4 sts.
16th row (K2, P2, K2, P4) 3 times, K2,

P4, K2, (P4, K2, P2, K2) 3 times, turn and cast on 6 sts.
17th row (P2, K4, P2, yon, sl 1, K1, psso) 3 times, P2, K4, P2, sl 1, K1, psso, K2 tog, P2, (K4, P2, yon, sl 1, K1, psso, P2) 3 times, turn and cast on 6 sts.
18th row (K2, P4, K2, P2) 7 times, K2, P4, K2, turn and cast on 4 sts.
19th row (P2, K2 tog, yrn, P2, K4) 8 times, P2, turn and cast on 4 sts.
20th row (K2, P2, K2, P4) 8 times, K2, P2, K2. 86 sts.
Mark each end of last row. Cont in patt as set, working C4 on next and every foll 6th row, until work measures 14cm *(5½in)* from markers, ending with a WS row. **.
Waistband
Next row (K1, P1) 12 times, patt 38, (P1, K1) to end.
Next row Rib 24, patt 38, rib 24.
Rep last row 8 times more.
Next row Rib 24, turn and leave rem sts on holder.
Cont in rib on these 24 sts for 8 more rows. Cast off in rib.
With RS of work facing, sl first 38 sts on to holder, rejoin yarn to rem 24 sts and rib to end. Work 8 more rows rib. Cast off in rib.
Bib
With RS of work facing, rejoin yarn to centre 38 sts and patt to end. Cont in patt until bib measures 8cm *(3¼in)* from beg, ending with a WS row and dec one st in centre of last row. 37 sts. Break off yarn.
Bib border
With RS of work facing, beg at waistband and K up 33 sts up left side of bib, work in K1, P1 rib across 37 sts, then K up 33 sts down right side of bib. 103 sts.
Next row K1, *P1, K1, rep from * to end.
Next row Rib 33, pick up loop lying between sts and K tbl – called inc 1 –, K1, inc 1, rib 35, inc 1, K1, inc 1, rib to end.
Next row Rib 32, K2, P1, K2, rib 33, K2, P1, K2, rib to end.
Next row Rib 34, inc 1, K1, inc 1, rib 37, inc 1, K1, inc 1, rib to end.
Next row Rib to end.
Cont in this way, inc on next and foll alt row. 119 sts. Work 3 more rows rib.
Next row Rib 34, P2 tog, K1, P2 tog, rib 41, P2 tog, K1, P2 tog, rib to end.
Cont to dec in this way, keeping rib correct over decs, on foll 3 alt rows. Cast off in rib.

Back
Work as given for front until 17th row has been completed. 78 sts.
18th row As given for front, omitting cast on 4 sts at end of row.
19th row (P2, K4, P2, K2 tog, yrn) 7 times, P2, K4, P2.
Cont in patt without shaping until work matches front to **.
Waistband
Next row K1, *P1, K1, rep from * to end. Work 18 more rows rib. Cast off in rib.

Straps (make 2)
Using No.12 needles cast on 13 sts.

1st row K1, *P1, K1, rep from * to end.
2nd row P1, *K1, P1, rep from * to end.
Rep these 2 rows until work measures 24cm
(*9½in*), or length required, from beg. Cast
off in rib.

To make up
Join side seams.

Leg borders Using No.11 needles and
with RS of work facing, K up 97 sts round
legs. Work 16 rows rib as given for straps.
Cast off loosely in rib.
Join crutch seam. Fold all ribbed borders
in half to WS and sl st in position. Sew on
straps inside ribbing at each side of top of
bib. Make a button loop at end of each

*Sun suit with buttoned straps for warm
days—put a sweater underneath when the
sun goes in.*

strap. Sew buttons to back waist. Thread
elastic through hem at back waist and draw
up to length required. Press seams under a
dry cloth with a cool iron.

Baby's embroidered coat

Sizes
To fit 46cm (18in) chest

Length to shoulder, 26cm (10¼in)
Sleeve seam, 18cm (7in)

Tension
30 sts and 38 rows to 10cm (3.9in) over st st worked on No.11 needles

Materials
5 x 25grm balls Patons Purple Heather 4 ply in main shade, A
1 ball or oddments in each of 3 contrasting colours, B, C and D
One pair No.11 needles

3 buttons

Back and fronts
Using No.11 needles and A, cast on 160 sts and work in one piece to underarm.

Below : Baby's coat with embroidered flowers and coloured edges knitted in. Below centre and right : Sleeveless dress with shoulder fastening and matching knickers.

K 10 rows. Beg with a P row, work 20 rows reverse st st.
Next row (RS) K3, P154, K3.
Next row P3, K154, P3.
Next row K6, P148, K6.
Next row P6, K148, P6
Next row K9, P142, K9.
Cont in this way, working 3 sts more in st st at each end of every alt row 10 times more. Cont in st st across all sts until work measures 15cm *(6in)* from beg, ending with a P row.

Divide for armholes
Next row K40 and leave these sts on holder for right front, K until there are 80 sts for back, turn and leave rem 40 sts on holder for left front.
Complete back first.
Next row P to end.
Next row K1, K2 tog, K to last 3 sts, sl 1, K1, psso, K1.
Rep these 2 rows 9 times more. 60 sts.
Cont without shaping until armholes measure 11cm *(4¼in)* from beg, ending with a P row.
Shape shoulders and neck
Next row Cast off 4 K, until there are 22 sts on right hand needle, turn and leave rem sts on holder.
Next row Cast off 5, P to end.
Next row Cast off 4, K to end.
Rep last 2 rows once more. P 1 row. Cast off rem 4 sts.
With RS of work facing, sl first 8 sts on holder for back neck, rejoin yarn to rem sts and K to end. Complete to match first side.
With WS of work facing, rejoin yarn to right front sts and P to end.
Next row K to last 3 sts, sl 1, K1, psso, K1.
Cont to dec in this way on every foll alt row 9 times more. 30 sts. Cont without shaping until armhole measures 8cm *(3¼in)* from beg, ending with a K row.
Shape neck
Next row P24, turn and leave rem 6 sts on holder.
Cast off 2 sts at beg of next and foll alt row. Dec one st at neck edge on foll 4 alt rows. 16 sts.
Shape shoulder
Cast off at beg of next and foll alt rows 4 sts 4 times
With RS of work facing, rejoin yarn to left front sts and K to end. Complete to match right front, reversing shaping.

Sleeves
Using No.11 needles, D and using the thumb method, cast on 44 sts. Break off D. Join in C and K 2 rows. Break off C. Join in B and K 2 rows. Break off B. Join in A and K 12 rows. Beg with a K row, cont in st st, inc one st at each end of first and every foll 6th row until there are 64 sts.
Cont without shaping until sleeve measures 18cm *(7in)* from beg, ending with a P row.
Shape top
Next row K1, K2 tog, K to last 3 sts, sl 1, K1, psso, K1.

Next row P to end.
Rep last 2 rows 9 times more. Cast off rem 44 sts.

To make up
Press under a damp cloth with a warm iron. Join shoulder seams. Join sleeve seams. Set in sleeves.
Border Using No.11 needles, A and with RS of work facing, beg at lower edge of right front and K up 2 sts up right front edge, 66 sts round neck (including sts on holders) and 62 sts down left front edge. 190 sts.
Next row K to end. Break off A. Join in B.
Next row (buttonhole row) Using B, K29, (cast off 2, K12) twice, cast off 2, K2, K twice into next st – called inc 1 –, K1, inc 1, K62, inc 1, K1, inc 1, K to end.
Next row K to end, casting on 2 sts over those cast off in previous row. Break off B. Join in C.
Next row Using C, K63, inc 1, K1, inc 1, K64, inc 1, K1, inc 1, K to end.
Next row K to end. Break off C. Join in D.
Next row Using D, K64, inc 1, K1, inc 1, K66, inc 1, K1, inc 1, K to end. Cast off.
Work embroidery as shown in photograph. Press seams. Sew on buttons to correspond with buttonholes.

Baby's dress & knickers

Sizes
To fit 46cm *(18in)* chest
Dress length to shoulder, 32cm *(12½in)*
Pants side seam, 15cm *(6in)*
Tension
24 sts and 32 rows to 10cm *(3.9in)* over st st worked on No.9 needles
Materials
8 x 25grm balls Patons Double Knitting
One pair No.9 needles
One No.3.00 (ISR) crochet hook
6 buttons
Waist length of elastic

Dress back
Using No.9 needles cast on 88 sts. Beg with a K row, cont in st st until work measures 20cm *(7¾in)* from beg, ending with a P row.
Shape armholes
Cast off at beg of next and every row 3 sts twice, 2 sts 4 times and one st twice. 72 sts.
Next row (RS) P1, *K1, P2, rep from * to last 2 sts, K1, P1.
Next row K1, *P1, K2, rep from * to last 2 sts, P1, K1.
Rep last 2 rows until armholes measure 12cm *(4¾in)* from beg, ending with a WS row.
Shape shoulders
Cast off at beg of next and every row 6 sts 6 times. Cast off rem 36 sts.

Front
Work as given for back until armholes measure 8cm *(3¼in)* from beg, ending with a WS row.
Shape neck
Next row Patt 32, turn and leave rem sts on holder.
Cast off at beg of next and every foll alt row 3 sts twice, 2 sts twice and one st 4 times. 18 sts. Cont without shaping until armhole measures same as back to shoulder, ending at armhole edge.
Shape shoulder
Cast off at beg of next and foll alt rows 6 sts 3 times.
With RS of work facing, rejoin yarn to rem sts, cast off 8, patt to end. Patt 1 row. Complete to match first side.

To make up
Smocking Thread length of yarn into a blunt ended needle. Insert needle into first K rib on 2nd row of yoke, join first and 2nd ribs, take needle to back of work and bring it out in the 2nd rib 3 rows up, join the 2nd and 3rd ribs, take needle to back of work and bring it out in the 3rd rib 3 rows down (ie. same row as before), join the 3rd and 4th ribs, cont in this way across work.
Beg again on first rib on 8th row. Work in this way until back and front yokes have been completed.
Press st st sections under a damp cloth with a warm iron. Join side seams.
Edging Using No.3.00 (ISR) hook and with RS of work facing, beg at top of left back armhole and work in dc round left armhole, across left front shoulder (making 3 button loops), round front neck, across right front shoulder (making 3 button loops), round right armhole, across right back shoulder, neck and left back shoulder. Do not turn. Work a row of crab st (ie. work in dc from left to right instead of from right to left) round edges.
Work 1 round dc and 1 round crab st round lower edge. Press seams. Sew 3 buttons to each back shoulder.

Pants back
Using No.9 needles cast on 16 sts. Beg with a K row, work 12 rows st st.
**Shape legs
Cast on at beg of next and every row one st 4 times, 2 sts 8 times and 10 sts twice. 56 sts. Mark each end of last row. Cont without shaping until work measures 18cm *(7in)* from markers. Cast off.

Front
Using No.9 needles cast on 16 sts. Beg with a K row, work 20 rows st st. Work as given for pants back from ** to end.

To make up
Press as given for dress. Join side and crutch seams. Turn 2cm *(¾in)* to WS at waist and 1cm *(½in)* round legs and sl st in position. Thread elastic through waist. Press seams.

Dressing gown with tie belt

Sizes
To fit 45.5[51:56:61]cm (18[20:22:24]in) chest
Length to shoulder, 57[61:65:68.5]cm (22½[24:25½:27]in)
Sleeve seam, 18[20.5:23:25.5]cm (7[8:9:10]in)
The figures in brackets [ ] refer to the 51 (20), 56 (22) and 61cm (24in) sizes respectively

Tension
16 sts and 22 rows to 10cm (3.9in) over st st worked on No.4 needles

Materials
7[8:9:11] x 50grm balls Wendy Naturelle in main shade, A
1 ball each of contrast colours, B, C and D
One pair No.3 needles
One pair No.4 needles
One pair No.5 needles
One No.5 circular Twin pin

Back and fronts
Using No.5 needles and A, cast on 91[101:111:121] sts and work in one piece to underarm. Beg with a K row, work 7 rows st st, ending with a K row.
Next row K to end to form hemline. Change to No.3 needles. Beg with a K row, cont in st st until work measures 25.5[28:30.5:33]cm (10[11:12:13]in) from hemline. Change to No.4 needles. Cont in st st until work measures 31.5[34.5:37:39.5]cm (12½[13½:14½:15½]in) from hemline, ending with a P row. Work 15 rows Fair Isle patt from chart, ending with a K row. Break off B, C and D. Using A, P 1 row.
Divide for back and front raglans
Next row K2 tog, K21[24:27:30], K2 tog, turn and leave rem sts on holder.
Complete right front first. Dec one st at each end of every foll alt row until 9[8:7:6] sts rem, ending with a P row.
Next row K to last 2 sts, K2 tog.
Next row P to end.
Rep last 2 rows until 2 sts rem, ending with a P row. K2 tog. Fasten off.
With RS of work facing, rejoin yarn to sts on holder, K2 tog, K37[41:45:49], K2 tog, turn and leave rem sts on holder. Complete back first. Dec one st at each end of every foll alt row until 11[13:15:17] sts rem, ending with a P row. Cast off.
With RS of work facing, rejoin yarn to sts on holder, K2 tog, K to last 2 sts, K2 tog.
Complete left front to match right front, reversing shaping.

Sleeves
Using No.5 needles and A, cast on 24[26:28:30] sts. Work 8 rows K1, P1 rib. Change to No.4 needles.
Next row K2[3:4:5], *K twice into next st — called inc 1 –, K1, rep from * to last 2[3:4:5] sts, inc 1, K1[2:3:4]. 35[37:39:41] sts.
Beg with a P row, work 13[17:21:25] rows st st, ending with a P row. Work 15 rows Fair Isle patt from chart. Break off B, C and D. Using A, P 1 row.
Shape raglan
Dec one st at each end of next and every foll alt row until 5 sts rem, ending with a P row. Cast off.

Collar and borders
Join raglan seams. Using No.5 needles and A, cast on 16[18:20:22] sts for back of collar. Work 1 row K1, P 1 rib. Cont in rib, cast on at beg of next and every row 8 sts 8 times and 6 sts twice. 92[94:96:98] sts. Break off yarn. Leave sts on holder. Using No.5 Twin pin, A and with RS of work facing, beg at hemline on right front and K up 70[72:74:76] sts along front to beg of shaping, rib across collar sts on holder and K up 70[72:74:76] sts down left front from beg of shaping to hemline. 232[238:244:250] sts. Rib 5 more rows. Cast off in rib.

Belt
Using No.5 needles and A, cast on 6 sts. Work in K1, P1 rib until belt measures 99[101.5:104:106.5]cm (39[40:41:42]in) from beg. Cast off in rib.

To make up
Press under a damp cloth with a warm iron. Join sleeve seams. Sew collar to neck edge. Turn hem at lower edge to WS and sl st in position. Press hem and sleeve seams.

Girl's crochet dressing gown

Sizes
To fit 45.5[53.5:61]cm (18[21:24]in) chest
Length to shoulder, 45.5[53.5:61]cm (18[21:24]in)
Sleeve seam, 15[18:21]cm (6[7:8¼]in)
The figures in brackets [ ] refer to the 53.5 (21) and 61cm (24in) sizes respectively

Tension
18 sts and 10 rows to 10cm (3.9in) over tr worked on No.4.00 (ISR) crochet hook

Materials
8[9:10] x 20grm balls of Wendy Courtellon Double Knitting in main shade, A
2[2:3] balls of contrast colour, B
1[1:2] balls each of contrast colours, C and D
One No.4.00 (ISR) crochet hook
One No.3.50 (ISR) crochet hook
5 buttons

Back and fronts
Using No.4.00 (ISR) hook and A, make 120[139:158]ch, beg at lower edge and work in one piece to underarm.

1st row Into 4th ch from hook work 1tr, 1tr into each ch to end. Turn. 118[137:156]tr.
2nd row 3ch to count as first tr, miss first tr, 1tr into each tr to end. Turn.
Rep 2nd row 4[6:8] times more.
Shape skirt
Next row 3ch, work 9[11:12]tr, *work 2tr tog, 22[26:30]tr, rep from * 3 times more, work 2tr tog, 10[11:13]tr. Turn. 113[132:151]sts.
Work 3 rows without shaping.
Next row 3ch, work 9[10:12]tr, *work 2tr tog, 21[25:29]tr, rep from * 3 times more, work 2tr tog, 9[11:12]tr. Turn. 108[127:146] sts.
Work 3 rows without shaping.
Next row 3ch, work 8[10:11]tr, *work 2tr tog, 20[24:28]tr, rep from * 3 times more, work 2tr tog, 9[10:12]tr. Turn. 103[122:141]sts.
Work 3 rows without shaping. Cont dec in this way on next and every foll 4th row until 88[102:116] sts rem. Cont without shaping until work measures 30[36:42]cm (11¾[14¼:16½]in) from beg.
Divide for armholes
Next row 3ch, work 18[21:24]tr, turn. Complete this front first. Dec one st at beg of next row and at same edge on next 2[3:4] rows. 16[18:20] sts. Cont without shaping until armhole measures 5[6:7]cm (2[2¼:2¾]in) from beg, ending at armhole edge.
Shape neck
Next row Patt to last 2[3:4] sts, turn.
Next row Ss over first 2 sts, patt to end. Turn.
Dec one st at neck edge on next 4 rows, then cont without shaping if necessary until armhole measures 11[12.5:14]cm (4¼[5:5½]in) from beg. Fasten off.
Return to where work was left, miss first 4[5:6] sts for underarm, rejoin yarn to next st, 3ch, work 41[47:53]tr, turn. Complete back. Dec one st at each end of next 3[4:5] rows. 36[40:44] sts. Cont without shaping until back measures same as front to shoulder. Fasten off.
Return to where work was left, miss first 4[5:6] sts for underarm, rejoin yarn to next st, 3ch, patt to end. Complete to match first front, reversing shaping.

Sleeves
Using No.4.00 (ISR) hook and A, make 31[34:37] ch. Work first 2 rows as given for back and fronts. 29[32:35]tr. Cont in tr, inc one st at each end of next and every foll 3rd row until there are 35[40:45]tr. Work 1 row.
Shape top
Next row Ss over first 2[3:3] sts, patt to last 2[3:3] sts, turn.
Dec one st at each end of next 4[5:5] rows, then 2 sts at each end of next 3[3:4] rows. 11[12:13] sts. Fasten off.

Pockets (make 2)
Using No.3.50 (ISR) hook and A, make 18ch.

1st row Into 3rd ch from hook work 1dc, 1dc into each ch to end. Break off A. 17dc.
2nd row With RS facing, join in B, 4ch, *miss 1dc, keeping last loop of each st on hook work 3tr into next dc, yrh and draw through all 4 loops on hook – called 1 Cl –, 1ch, rep from * 6 times more, miss 1dc, 1tr into last dc. Break off B.
3rd row With RS facing, join in C, 3ch, 1 Cl into first 1 ch sp, *1ch, miss 1 dc, 1 Cl into next dc, rep from * 6 times more, 1tr into top of tr of last row. Break off C.
4th row With RS facing, join in D, 4ch, miss first 1 Cl, *1 Cl into next 1ch sp, 1ch, rep from * 6 times more, 1tr into top of tr of last row. Break off D.
Rep 3rd, 4th and 3rd rows once more, working in B, C and D. With RS of work facing, join in B, 1ch, work 1dc into each dc to end, then work a row of crab st, working in dc from left to right instead of from right to left. Fasten off.

To make up
Press lightly under a dry cloth with a cool iron. Join shoulder and sleeve seams. Set in sleeves.
Edging Using No.3.50 (ISR) hook, A and with RS of work facing, rejoin yarn at centre back of lower edge and work in dc right round edges, working 1dc into each st along lower edge and approx 3dc into every 2 rows up front edge. Join with a ss to first dc. Break off A.
Next round With RS facing, join in B to ss, 4ch, miss 1dc, *1 Cl into next dc ,1ch, miss 1dc, rep from * all round, inc at each corner at bottom and top of front edges by working (1 Cl, 1ch, 1 Cl) into dc at corners. Join with a ss to 3rd of first 4ch. Break off B.
Next round Join in C to ss at end of last round, 3ch, 1 Cl into first 1ch sp, *1ch,

Storytime dressing gowns make bedtimes a treat. Left : Knitted, wrapover dressing gown with tie belt. Right : Crochet button-through dressing gown.

1 Cl into next 1ch sp, rep from * all round, inc at corners as before. Break off C.
Next round Join in D to ss at end of last round, 4ch, 1 Cl into next 1ch sp, noting that this is after the first 1 Cl in C, *1ch, 1 Cl into next 1ch sp, rep from * all round, inc at corners as before. Break off D.
Next round Join in B to ss at end of last round, 1ch, *1dc into 1ch sp, 1dc into 1 Cl, rep from * all round, still inc at corners. Join with a ss to first 1ch.
Do not turn but work a row of crab st all round, as given for pockets. Fasten off.
Work round sleeve edges in same way. Sew on pockets. Sew on buttons, using holes in border for buttonholes.

23

Ribbed boiler suit & cap

Sizes
To fit 51[56]cm *(20[22]in)* chest

Neck to crutch, 49[54]cm *(19¼[21¼]in)*
Inside leg seam, 31[36]cm *(12¼[14¼]in)*
Sleeve seam, 24[28]cm *(9½[11]in)*
including cuff
The figures in brackets [ ] refer to the
56cm *(22in)* size only

Tension
24 sts and 32 rows to 10cm *(3.9in)* over st
st worked on No.9 needles

Materials
Blarney Tivoleen
Suit 16[18] x 25grm balls in main shade, A
1[2] balls of contrast colour, B
One pair No.9 needles
50cm *(20in)* zip fastener
Cap 2[2] balls in main shade, A
Oddments of contrast colour, B
One pair No.10 needles

Suit right half

Using No.9 needles and A, cast on 86[94] sts.

1st row (RS) K2, *P2, K2, rep from * to end.

2nd row P2, *K2, P2, rep from * to end.

Rep these 2 rows until work measures 21[24]cm *(8¼[9½]in)* from beg, ending with a WS row. Join in B. Rib 2 rows B, 2 rows A and 6 rows B. Break off B. Cont in rib and A only, inc one st at each end of next and every foll 6th[8th] row until there are 94[102] sts. Cont without shaping until work measures 31[36]cm *(12¼[14¼]in)* from beg, ending with a WS row.

Shape crutch

Cast off at beg of next and every row 3 sts once, 4 sts once, 2 sts once, 3 sts once, one st once and 2 sts twice. Dec one st at end of next and foll 2 alt rows. 76[84] sts. Cont without shaping until work measures 30[33]cm *(11¾[13]in)* from beg of crutch shaping, ending with a WS row. Join in B. Rib 2 rows B, 2 rows A and 6 rows B. Break off B. Rib 12 more rows A.

Divide for armhole

Next row K38[42], turn and leave rem sts on holder.

Complete front first. Cast off at beg of next and foll alt rows 3 sts once, 2 sts once and one st 1[3] times. 32[34] sts. Cont without shaping until armhole measures 8[10]cm *(3¼[4]in)* from beg, ending at front edge.

Shape neck

Cast off at beg of next and foll alt rows 8[10] sts once, 2 sts twice and one st twice. 18 sts. Cont without shaping until armhole measures 12[14]cm *(4¾[5½]in)* from beg, ending with a WS row. Cast off.

With RS of work facing, rejoin yarn to rem sts, cast off 3, rib to end. Cont on these sts for half back. Cast off at beg of foll alt rows 2 sts once and one st 1[3] times. 32[34] sts. Cont without shaping until armhole measures 10[12]cm *(4[4¾]in)* from beg, ending at centre back edge.

Shape neck

Cast off at beg of next and foll alt rows 8[10] sts once and 2 sts 3 times. Cast off rem 18 sts.

Suit left half

Work to match right half, reversing all shaping.

Sleeves

Using No.9 needles and A, cast on 54[58] sts. Work 8cm *(3¼in)* rib as given for suit right half. Cont in rib, inc one st at each end of next and every foll 6th row until there are 64[68] sts. Cont without shaping until sleeve measures 24[28]cm *(9½[11]in)* from beg, ending with a WS row.

Shape top

Cast off at beg of next and every row 4 sts twice, 3 sts twice, 2 sts twice, one st 6[10] times, 4 sts twice, 5 sts twice and 22 sts

Warm in winter—a ribbed boilersuit and cap with double stripes (left) and polo-necked jersey to match (right).

once.

Neckband

Join shoulder seams. Using No.9 needles, A and with RS of work facing, K up 70[78] sts evenly round neck. Work 12cm *(4¾in)* rib. Cast off in rib.

To make up

Do not press. Join sleeve seams. Set in sleeves. Join inside leg seams. Fold neckband in half to WS and sl st in position. Sew in zip. Join rem front seam below zip.

Cap

Using No.10 needles and A, cast on 108[120] sts. Beg with a K row, cont in st st until work measures 12[13]cm *(4¾[5]in)* from beg, ending with a P row. Join in B. Cont in st st, work 2 rows B, 2 rows A and 6 rows B. Break off B. Cont in A for a further 5[6]cm *(2[2¼]in)*, ending with a P row.

Shape top

Next row K1, K2 tog, K49[55], sl 1, K1, psso, K2 tog, K49[55], sl 1, K1, psso, K1.

Next row P to end.

Next row K1, K2 tog, K47[53], sl 1, K1, psso, K2 tog, K47[53], sl 1, K1, psso, K1.

Cont to dec 4 sts in this way on every foll alt row until 60[64] sts rem. Cast off.

To make up

Press under a damp cloth with a warm iron. Join top seam. Join side seam. Fold lower part to inside so that cast on edge is level with beg of first stripe and sl st in position. Press seams.

Jersey with double stripe

Sizes

To fit 51[56]cm *(20[22]in)* chest

Length to shoulder, 35[40]cm *(13¾[15¾]in)*

Sleeve seam, 24[28]cm *(9½[11]in)* including cuff

The figures in brackets [ ] refer to the 56cm *(22in)* size only

Tension

24 sts and 32 rows to 10cm *(3.9in)* over st st worked on No.9 needles

Materials

9[11] x 25grm balls Blarney Tivoleen in main shade, A

1 ball of contrast colour, B

One pair No.9 needles

Back and front

Using No.9 needles and A, cast on 154[170] sts and work in one piece to underarm.

1st row (RS) K2, *P2, K2, rep from * to end.

2nd row P2, *K2, P2, rep from * to end.

Rep these 2 rows until work measures 15[18]cm *(6[7]in)* from beg, ending with a

WS row. Join in B. Rib 2 rows B, 2 rows A and 6 rows B. Break off B. Rib 12 more rows A.

Divide for armholes

Next row Cast off 4, rib 73[81], turn and leave rem sts on holder.

Complete back first.

Next row Cast off 3, rib to end. 70[78] sts. Cast off at beg of next and every row 2 sts 2[4] times and one st 4 times. 62[66] sts. Cont without shaping until armholes measure 12[14]cm *(4¾[5½]in)* from beg, ending with a WS row.

Shape shoulders and neck

Next row Rib 17[18], turn and leave rem sts on holder.

Complete this shoulder first.

Next row Rib to end.

Next row Cast off 5, rib to last 2 sts, K2 tog. Rep last 2 rows once more, then first of them again. Cast off rem 5[6] sts.

With RS of work facing, rejoin yarn to rem sts at neck, cast off 28[30], rib to end. Complete to match first shoulder.

With RS of work facing, rejoin yarn to rem sts for front, cast off 3, rib to end.

Next row Cast off 4, rib to end. 70[78] sts. Cast off at beg of next and every row 2 sts 2[4] times and one st 4 times. 62[66] sts. Cont without shaping until armholes measure 10[12]cm *(4[4¾]in)* from beg, ending with a WS row.

Shape neck

Next row Rib 19[20], turn and leave rem sts on holder.

Complete this side first. Dec one st at neck edge on every foll alt row until 15[16] sts rem. Cont without shaping until armhole measures same as back to shoulder, ending at armhole edge.

Shape shoulder

Cast off at beg of next and foll alt rows 5 sts twice and 5[6] sts once.

With RS of work facing, rejoin yarn to rem sts, cast off 24[26], rib to end. Complete to match first side.

Sleeves

Using No.9 needles and A, cast on 54[58] sts. Work 8cm *(3¼in)* rib as given for back and front. Cont in rib, inc one st at each end of next and every roll 6th row until there are 64[68] sts. Cont without shaping until sleeve measures 24[28]cm *(9½[11]in)* from beg, ending with a WS row.

Shape top

Cast off at beg of next and every row 4 sts twice, 3 sts twice, 2 sts twice, one st 6[10] times, 4 sts twice, 5 sts twice and 22 sts once.

Neckband

Join right shoulder seam. Using No.9 needles, A and with RS of work facing, K up 74[86] sts evenly round neck. Work 12cm *(4¾in)* rib. Cast off in rib.

To make up

Do not press. Join left shoulder and neckband seam. Join right side seam. Join sleeve seams. Set in sleeves.

Stripey pram set with all~in~one suit

Sizes
To fit 45.5[51]cm *(18[20]in)* chest
Length from front neck to crutch,
31.5[35]cm *(12½[13¾]in)*
Inside leg to ankle 20[23]cm *(7¾[9]in)*
Sleeve seam, 15[18]cm *(6[7]in)*
Blanket 70cm *(27½in)* long by 51cm *(20in)* wide
The figures in brackets [ ] refer to the 51cm *(20in)* size only

Tension
28 sts and 36 rows to 10cm *(3.9in)* over st st worked on No.10 needles; 28 sts and 52 rows to 10cm *(3.9in)* over g st worked on No.10 needles

Materials
Suit 2[3] x 20grm balls Sirdar Wash 'n' Wear 4 ply in main shade, A
2[2] balls each of contrast colours, B and C
Bonnet and mitts 1 ball of A
1 ball each of B and C
Blanket 4 balls in A
3 balls each of B and C
One pair No.10 needles
One pair No.12 needles
One No.2.50 (ISR) crochet hook
25[30]cm *(10[12]in)* zip fastener

Suit
Using No.12 needles and A, cast on 39[43] sts loosely and beg with left leg.
1st row K1, *P1, K1, rep from * to end.
2nd row P1, *K1, P1, rep from * to end.
Rep these 2 rows 3 times more. Change to No.10 needles. Beg with a K row cont in st st, working throughout in stripes of 6 rows B, 6 rows C and 6 rows A, *at the same time* inc one st at each end of 7th and every foll 4th row until there are 61[69] sts. Work 3 rows without shaping. Inc one st at each end of next and foll 5 alt rows, then cast on 2 sts at beg of next 4 rows. 81[89] sts.
Break off yarn and leave sts on holder.
Work right leg in same way. Do not break off yarn.

Join legs
Next row K across right leg to last st, K last st tog with first st of left leg, K across

A striking, stripey pram set for a lively baby – he'll stand out in a crowd with this neat, all-in-one suit, bonnet (when Big Dog isn't wearing it!), mittens and blanket.

left leg. 161[177] sts.
Keeping striped sequence correct, cont in st st and work 3 rows.

Shape crutch

Next row K78[86], sl 1, K1, psso, K1, K2 tog, K to end.
Cont dec in this way in centre of every 4th row 8[9] times more. 143[157] sts. Cont without shaping until work measures 24.5[27]cm *(9¾[10¾]in)* from join, ending with a P row.

Divide for armholes

Next row K33[36], cast off 7[8], K63[69], cast off 7[8], K to end.
Complete left front first.
Next row P to end.
Next row K1, K2 tog, K to end.
Rep last 2 rows until 21[22] sts rem, ending with a P row.

Shape neck

Next row K1, K2 tog, K15, turn and leave rem 3[4] sts on holder.
Next row Cast off 2, P to end.
Next row K1, K2 tog, K to last 2 sts, K2 tog.
Next row P to end.
Rep last 2 rows 5 times more.
Next row K1, K2 tog.
Next row P2 tog. Fasten off.
With WS of work facing, rejoin yarn to 63[69] sts for back and P to end.
Next row K1, K2 tog, K to last 3 sts, sl 1, K1, psso, K1.
Next row P to end.
Rep last 2 rows until 23[25] sts rem, ending with a P row. Leave sts on holder.
With WS of work facing, rejoin yarn to rem 33[36] sts and P to end.
Next row K to last 3 sts, sl 1, K1, psso, K1.
Complete to match left front, reversing shaping.

Sleeves

Using No.12 needles and A, cast on 41[45] sts. Work 8 rows rib as given for leg. Change to No.12 needles. Beg with a K row cont in st st and striped sequence as given for body, inc one st at each end of first and every foll 6th row until there are 57[63] sts. Cont without shaping until sleeve measures 15[18] cm *(6[7]in)* from beg, ending with same patt row as armholes of body, noting that you can work out which colour stripe to beg with by measuring the sleeve length against the body from the armhole downwards.

Shape top

Cast off 4 sts at beg of next 2 rows.
Next row K1, K2 tog, K to last 3 sts, sl 1, K1, psso, K1.
Next row P to end.
Rep last 2 rows until 9[11] sts rem, ending with a P row.
Leave sts on holder.

Neckband

Join raglan seams. Using No.12 needles, A and with RS of work facing, K across 3[4] sts of right front neck, K up 16 sts up neck, K across sts of right sleeve, back neck and left sleeve, K2 tog at each back raglan seam,

K up 16 sts down front neck then K across rem 3[4] sts of left front neck. 77[85] sts.
Work 12 rows rib as given for leg. Cast off loosely in rib. Fold neckband in half to WS and sl st down.

Left foot

Using No.12 needles, A and with RS of work facing, K up 39[43] sts from cast on edge.
Next row K21[22], change to No.10 needles, P13[15], turn.
**Cont in st st on these 13[15] sts and work 6 rows C, 6 rows B, 6 rows A.
Next row Using C, K1, sl 1, K1, psso, K to last 3 sts, K2 tog, K1.
Next row P to end.
Rep last 2 rows twice more. 7[9] sts.
Break off yarn. **.
Using No.12 needles, A and with WS of work facing, rejoin yarn to 5[6] sts which were left and K to end.
Next row K5[6], K up 16 sts along side of foot, K 7[9] toe sts, K up 16 sts along other side of foot, then K21[22] sts. 65[69] sts.
K 8[12] rows g st.
Next row K6, K2 tog, K1, K2 tog, K27[29], K2 tog, K1, K2 tog, K22[24].
Next row K to end.
Next row K5, K2 tog, K1, K2 tog, K25[27], K2 tog, K1, K2 tog, K21[23].
Next row K to end.
Next row K4, K2 tog, K1, K2 tog, K23[25], K2 tog, K1, K2 tog, K20[22].
Next row K to end.
Cast off.

Right foot

Using No.12 needles, A and with RS of work facing, K up 39[43] sts from cast on edge.
Next row K5[6], change to No.10 needles, P13[15], turn.
Rep from ** to ** as given for left foot.
Using No.12 needles A and with WS of work facing, rejoin yarn to 21[22] sts and K to end.
Next row K21[22], K up 16 sts along side of foot, K7[9] toe sts, K up 16 sts along other side of foot, K5[6]. 65[69] sts.
K8[12] rows g st.
Next row K22[24], K2 tog, K1, K2 tog, K27[29], K2 tog, K1, K2 tog, K6.
Complete to match left foot, reversing shaping as shown.

To make up

Press each piece under a dry cloth with a cool iron. Join sleeve seams. Join leg and foot seams. Using No.2.50 (ISR) hook, A and with RS of work facing, work 1 row dc along each side of front opening. Sew in zip, joining rem part of seam below zip. Press seams.

Bonnet

Using No.12 needles and A, cast on 91 sts. Work 8 rows rib as given for leg. Change to No.10 needles. Beg with a K row cont in st st, working (6 rows each in B, C and A) twice. 36 rows in all.

Shape crown

1st row Keeping striped patt correct, *K8, K2 tog, rep from * to last st, K1.
2nd row P to end.
3rd row *K7, K2 tog, rep from * to last st, K1.
4th row P to end.
Cont dec in this way on next and every alt row until 19 sts rem, ending with a P row.
Next row *K2 tog, rep from * to last st, K1. 10 sts.
Next row P to end.
Break off yarn, thread through rem sts, draw up and fasten off securely.

To make up

Press as given for suit. Join back seam from top to beg of crown shaping. Using No.2.50 (ISR) hook, A and with RS of work facing, work 2 rows dc round neck edge. Using A, make 2 twisted cords and sew one to each corner.

Mitts

Using No.12 needles and A, cast on 35 sts and work 4cm *(1½in)* rib as given for leg, ending with a WS row.
Next row (eyelet holes) K1, *yfwd, K2 tog, rep from * to end.
Next row Rib to end.
Change to No.10 needles. Beg with a K row cont in st st, working 6 rows in A, 6 in B, 6 in C, then 4 in A.

Shape top

1st row Keeping striped patt correct, *K1, sl 1, K1, psso, K12, K2 tog, rep from * once more, K1.
2nd row P to end.
3rd row *K1, sl 1, K1, psso, K10, K2 tog, rep from * once more, K1.
Cont dec in this way on alt rows twice more, ending with a K row. 19 sts.
Next row P2 tog, P8, fold work in half and graft sts tog.

To make up

Press as given for suit. Join seam. Press seams. Using A, make a twisted cord and thread through eyelet holes at wrist.

Blanket centre

Using No.10 needles and C, cast on 130 sts and work in g st throughout and striped sequence of (8 rows C, 8 rows A, 8 rows B) 14 times, then 8 rows C.
Cast off.

Border

Using No.10 needles and A, cast on 9 sts.
1st and 2nd rows Sl 1, K to end.
3rd row Sl 1, K5, turn.
4th row Sl 1, K to end.
Rep these 4 rows until shorter edge of border is long enough to fit right round centre of blanket.
Cast off.

To make up

Do not press. Sew shorter edge of border to centre, easing round corners, then join cast on and cast off edges of border.

Yoked jacket with lazy daisies

Sizes
To fit 43cm (17in) chest
Length to shoulder, 22cm (8¾in)
Sleeve seam, 16cm (6¼in)

Tension
30 sts and 60 rows to 10cm (3.9in) over g st
worked on No.11 needles

Materials
5 x 25grm balls Sirdar Superwash Wool
4 ply
One pair No.11 needles
One pair No.12 needles
Oddments of wool or silk for embroidery

Front and backs
Using No.11 needles cast on 144 sts. Work
15cm (6in) g st.

Divide for armholes
Next row K36, turn and leave rem sts on
holder. Complete left back first.
Next row K to end.
Next row K to last 3 sts, K2 tog, K1.

Rep last 2 rows 6 times more. 29 sts. K 1
row. Leave sts on holder.
With RS of work facing, rejoin yarn to rem
sts and K72, turn and leave rem sts on
holder. Cont on 72 sts for front.
**Next row K to end.
Next row K1, sl 1, K1, psso, K to last 3
sts, K2 tog, K1.
Rep least 2 rows 6 times more. **. 58 sts.
K 1 row. Leave sts on holder.
With RS of work facing, rejoin yarn to rem
sts and K to end.
Next row K to end.
Next row K1, sl 1, K1, psso, K to end.
Rep last 2 rows 6 times more. 29 sts. K 1
row. Leave sts on holder.

Sleeves
Using No.12 needles cast on 45 sts.
1st row (RS) K1, *P1, K1, rep from * to
end.
2nd row P1, *K1, P1, rep from * to end.
Rep these 2 rows until work measures 5cm
(2in) from beg, ending with a 2nd row.
Change to No.11 needles. Cont in g st, inc
one st at each end of first and every foll 8th
row until there are 61 sts. Cont without
shaping until sleeve measures 16cm (6¼in)
from beg, ending with a RS row.

Shape top
Work as given from ** to ** for front

*Pretty jacket with embroidered lazy daisies
round the yoke, plus crochet pram cover in
square motifs (see overleaf).*

armhole shaping. 47 sts. K 1 row. Leave sts
on holder.

Yoke
Using No.11 needles and with RS of work
facing, K across sts of left back, left sleeve,
front, right sleeve and right back, K2 tog
at each seam. 206 sts.
Next row P2, *P2 tog, P6, rep from * to
last 4 sts, P2 tog, P2. 180 sts.
Beg with a K row, work 7 rows st st.
Next row P2, *P2 tog, P4, rep from * to last
4 sts, P2 tog, P2. 150 sts.
Beg with a K row, work 7 rows st st.
Next row K4, *K2 tog, K3, rep from * to
last st, K1. 121 sts.
K 6 rows g st. Change to No.12 needles.
Work 14 rows rib as given for sleeves. Cast
off loosely in rib.

To make up
Do not press. Join raglan seams. Join side
and sleeve seams. Turn 4 rows of rib at
neck to WS and sl st in position. Make a
twisted cord approx 80cm (31½in) long and
thread through neck. Work embroidery on
yoke as shown in picture.

29

Crochet pram cover in square motifs

Size
42cm (16½in) wide x 48cm (19in) long
Tension
One motif measures 6cm (2¼in) square using No.4.00 (ISR) hook
Materials
3 x 25grm balls Sirdar Fontein Crepe in main shade, A
2 balls of contrast colour, B
1 ball of contrast colour, C
One No.3.50 (ISR) crochet hook
One No.4.00 (ISR) crochet hook

Motif
Using No.4.00 (ISR) hook and C, make 4 ch. Join with a ss into first ch to form a circle.
1st round 3ch to count as first tr, 11tr into circle. Join with a ss into 3rd of 3ch. Break off C.
2nd round Join in B between 2tr, 5ch, 3tr into same place, *miss 3tr, (3tr, 2ch and 3tr) into next sp between tr, rep from * twice more, miss 3tr, 2tr into same place as join. Join with a ss into 3rd of 5ch. Break off B.
3rd round Join in A to 2ch sp at corner, 5ch, 3tr into same sp, *3tr into sp between groups of tr, (3tr, 2ch and 3tr) into next 2ch sp at corner, rep from * twice more, 3tr into sp between groups of tr, 2tr into same place as join. Join with a ss into 3rd of 5ch.
Fasten off.
Make 41 more motifs. Join into 7 strips with 6 in each, then join strips together.

Border
Using No.3.50 (ISR) hook, A and with RS of work facing, rejoin yarn to one corner, 1ch, 1dc into same sp, *1dc into each of next 9tr, 1dc into sp at corner, 1dc into sp at corner of next motif, rep from * along one side to last motif, 1dc into each of next 9tr, 3dc into corner sp, cont in same way all round outer edge, ending with 1dc into same sp as join. Join with a ss into first ch.
Next round 1ch, 1dc into st at base of ch, 1dc into each of next 4dc, *3ch, miss 2dc, 1dc into each of next 9dc, rep from * along side to last motif, 3ch, miss 3dc, 1dc into each of next 5dc, 3dc into corner dc, 1dc into each of next 4dc, cont in same way all round, ending with 1dc into same place as first ch. Join with a ss into first ch.
Next round 1ch, 1dc into st at base of ch, *into next 3ch sp work (1dtr, 1ch) 10 times, 1dtr, miss 4dc, 1dc into next dc, rep from * along side, working 3dc into corner dc, cont all round work, ending with 1dc into same place as first ch. Join with a ss into first ch. Fasten off.

Polo~neck jerseys, plain or striped

Sizes
To fit 45.5[51:56:61]cm (18[20:22:24]in) chest
Length to shoulder, 25.5[29:33:37]cm (10[11½:13:14½]in)
Sleeve seam, 18[20.5:23:25.5]cm (7[8:9:10]in)
The figures in brackets [ ] refer to the 51 (20), 56 (22) and 61cm (24in) sizes respectively
Tension
32 sts and 38 rows to 10cm (3.9in) over rib worked on No.10 needles
Materials
Plain jersey 3[4:4:5] x 25grm balls Lister Lavenda 3 ply Wool or 4[5:5:6] x 20grm balls Lister Baby 3 ply Courtelle Nylon
Striped jersey 3 [3:4:4] balls Lister Lavenda 3 ply Wool or 3[3:4:4] balls Lister Baby 3 ply Courtelle Nylon in main shade, A
2[3:3:3] balls Lister Lavenda 3 ply Wool or 2[3:3:3] balls Lister Baby 3 ply Courtelle Nylon in contrast colour, B
One pair No.10 needles
One pair No.12 needles

Plain jersey back
Using No.10 needles cast on 73[81:89:97] sts.
1st row (RS) K1, *P1, K1, rep from * to end.
2nd row P1, *K1, P1, rep from * to end. These 2 rows form rib. Rep them until work measures 15[18:20.5:23]cm (6[7:8:9]in) from beg, ending with a WS row.
Shape armholes
Cast off 2[3:4:5] sts at beg of next 2 rows. Dec one st at each end of every row until 57[61:65:69] sts rem. **. Cont in rib without shaping until armholes measure 10[11.5:12.5:14]cm (4[4½:5:5½]in) from beg, ending with a WS row.
Shape shoulders
Cast off at beg of next and every row 7[8:8:9] sts twice and 8[8:9:9] sts twice. Leave rem 27[29:31:33] sts on holder for back neck.

Front
Work as given for back to **. Cont in rib without shaping until armholes measure 6.5[7.5:7.5:9]cm (2½[3:3:3½]in) from beg, ending with a WS row.
Divide for neck
Next row Rib 20[21:22:23], K2 tog, turn and leave rem sts on holder.
Complete this side first. Keeping armhole edge straight, dec one st at neck edge on every foll alt row until 15[16:17:18] sts rem. Cont without shaping until front

measures same as back to shoulder, ending at armhole edge.
Shape shoulder
Cast off at beg of next and foll alt row 7[8:8:9] sts once and 8[8:9:9] sts once. With RS of work facing, sl first 13[15:17:19] sts on to holder for centre front neck, rejoin yarn to next st, K2 tog, rib to end. Complete to match first side.

Sleeves
Using No.12 needles cast on 41[43:45:47] sts. Work 2.5cm (1in) rib as given for back. Change to No.10 needles. Cont in rib, inc one st at each end of next and every foll 6th row until there are 61[65:69:73] sts. Cont without shaping until sleeve measures 18[20.5:23:25.5]cm (7[8:9:10]in) from beg, ending with a WS row.
Shape top
Cast off 2[3:4:5] sts at beg of next 2 rows. Dec one st at each end of next and every foll 4th row until 53 sts rem, then at each end of every row until 9 sts rem. Cast off.

Polo collar
Join right shoulder seam. Using No.12 needles and with RS of work facing, K up 22[22:26:26] sts down left front neck, rib across centre front neck sts on holder, K up 22[22:26:26] sts up right front neck and rib across back neck sts on holder. 84[88:100:104] sts. Work 2.5cm (1in) K1, P1 rib. Change to No.10 needles. Work 5cm (2in) more rib. Cast off loosely.

To make up
Join left shoulder and collar seam. Set in sleeves. Join side and sleeve seams. Press seams.

Striped jersey back
Using No.10 needles and A, cast on 73[81:89:97] sts. Work 4 rows rib as given for plain jersey back. Using B, K 1 row. Using B, rib 3 rows. Using A, K 1 row. Using A, rib 3 rows. The last 8 rows form striped patt. Complete as given for plain jersey back, working in striped patt throughout.

Front
Work as given for plain jersey front, working in striped patt throughout.

Sleeves
Work as given for plain jersey sleeves, working first 2.5cm (1in) in A and ending with same stripe as back and front at underarm.

Polo collar
Using A throughout, work as given for plain jersey collar.

To make up
Complete as given for plain jersey.

Right : Bright little polo-necked jerseys to knit in a plain colour or simple two-colour stripes.

Baby's pullover & pants

Sizes
To fit 46[51]cm *(18[20]in)* chest
Jersey length to shoulder, 31[35]cm
(12¼[13¾]in)
Pants side seam, 21[23]cm *(8¼[9]in)*
The figures in brackets [ ] refer to the
51cm *(20in)* size only
Tension
24 sts and 32 rows to 10cm *(3.9in)* over st

st worked on No.9 needles
Materials
4[5] x 25grm balls Sunbeam Hyland
Superwash Double Knitting in main
shade, A
3[4] balls of contrast colour, B
One pair No.9 needles
One pair No.11 needles
Set of 4 No.11 needles pointed at both ends

Waist length of elastic for pants

Jersey front
Using No.11 needles and A, cast on 58[66] sts.
1st row (RS) K0[2], *P2, K2, rep from * to last 2[0] sts, P2[0].
2nd row P0[2], *K2, P2, rep from * to last 2[0] sts, K2[0].
Rep last 2 rows throughout, working in stripe sequence of 2 rows B and 2 rows A. Cont until work measures 20[23]cm (7¾[9]in) from beg, ending with a WS row.
Shape armholes
Cast off at beg of next and every row 3 sts twice, 2 sts 2[4] times and one st 6 times. 42[46] sts.
**Shape neck
Next row Rib 16, turn and leave rem sts on holder.
Complete this side first. Cast off at beg of next and foll alt rows 3 sts once, 2 sts once and one st once. 10 sts. Cont without shaping until armhole measures 11[12]cm (4¼[4¾]in) from beg, ending with a WS row. Cast off.
With RS of work facing, sl first 10[14] sts on holder for front neck, rejoin yarn to next st and rib to end. Complete to match first side.

Jersey back
Work as given for front until armhole shaping is completed. Cont without shaping until armholes measure 6[7]cm (2¼[2¾]in) from beg, ending with a WS row. Work as given for front from ** to end.

Neckband
Join shoulder seams. Using set of 4 No.11 needles, A and with RS of work facing, rib across back neck sts, K up 12 sts up left back neck, 26 sts down left front neck, rib across front neck sts, K up 26 sts up right front neck and 12 sts down right back neck. 96[104] sts. Work 3 rounds K2, P2 rib. Cast off in rib.

Armbands
Using No.11 needles, A and with RS of work facing, K up 58[66] sts round armholes. Beg with a 2nd row, work 3 rows rib as given for front. Cast off in rib.

To make up
Do not press. Join side seams. If necessary, press seams under a damp cloth with a warm iron, taking care not to flatten rib.

Pants left half
Using No.11 needles and A, cast on 50[58] sts. Work 3cm (1¼in) rib as given for jersey front, ending with a 2nd row. Change to No.9 needles. Cont in rib and stripe sequence as given for jersey, inc one

Far left : Baby's sleeveless pullover and pants set to knit in two colours.
Left : Smart short-sleeved sweater for active boys and girls.

st at each end of next and every foll alt row until there are 58[66] sts. Cont without shaping until work measures 6cm (2¼in) from beg, ending with a WS row.
Shape crutch
Dec one st at each end of next and foll 3[5] alt rows. 50[54] sts. Cont without shaping until work measures 19[21]cm (7½[8¼]in) from beg, ending with a WS row. Change to No.11 needles. Using A, rib 4cm (1½in). Cast off loosely in rib.

Pants right half
Work as given for left half.

To make up
Do not press. Join back and front seams. Join leg seams. Fold waistband in half to WS and sl st in position. If necessary, press seams as given for jersey. Thread elastic through waist.

Short-sleeved sweater

Sizes
To fit 51[56]cm (20[22]in) chest
Length to shoulder, 27[32]cm (10¾[12½]in)
Sleeve seam, 5[6]cm (2[2¼]in)
The figures in brackets [ ] refer to the 56cm (22in) size only
Tension
24 sts and 32 rows to 10cm (3.9in) over st st worked on No.9 needles
Materials
4[5] x 25grm balls Sunbeam Hyland Superwash Double Knitting in main shade, A
1 ball of contrast colour, B
One pair No.9 needles
One pair No.11 needles
2 buttons

Back
Using No.11 needles and A, cast on 67[73] sts.
1st row K1, *P1, K1, rep from * to end.
2nd row P1, *K1, P1, rep from * to end.
Rep these 2 rows until work measures 3cm (1¼in) from beg, ending with a 2nd row. Change to No.9 needles. Beg with a K row, cont in st st, working 28[38] rows A, 1 row B, 1 row A, 12 rows B, 1 row A, 1 row B and 2 rows A. Break off B. Cont using A only.
Shape armholes
Cast off 3 sts at beg of next 2 rows and 2 sts at beg of foll 2 rows. Dec one st at each end of next and foll 1[2] alt rows. 53[57] sts.
**. Work 1[5] rows without shaping, ending with a P row.
Divide for opening
Next row K25[27], K2 tog, turn and leave rem sts on holder.
Complete right back first.

Next row K2, P to end.
Next row K to end.
Rep last 2 rows until armhole measures 10[12]cm (4[4¾]in) from beg, ending at armhole edge.
Shape shoulder
Cast off at beg of next and foll alt rows 5 sts twice and 5[6] sts once. Leave rem 11[12] sts on holder.
With RS of work facing, rejoin yarn to sts on holder and K to end.
Next row P to last 2 sts, K2.
Complete to match first side.

Front
Work as given for back to **. Cont without shaping until armholes measure 6[8]cm (2¼[3¼]in) from beg, ending with a P row.
Shape neck
Next row K23[24], turn and leave rem sts on holder.
Complete this side first. Cast off 3 sts at beg of next row and 2 sts at beg of foll alt row. Dec one st at beg of next and foll 2 alt rows. 15[16] sts. Cont without shaping until armhole measures same as back to shoulder, ending at armhole edge.
Shape shoulder
Cast off at beg of next and foll alt rows 5 sts twice and 5[6] sts once.
With RS of work facing, sl first 7[9] sts on holder for front neck, rejoin yarn to next st and K to end. P 1 row. Complete to match first side.

Sleeves
Using No.11 needles and A, cast on 43[47] sts. Work 2cm (1¼in) rib as given for back, ending with a 2nd row. Change to No.9 needles. Beg with a K row, cont in st st, inc one st at each end of first and every foll 2nd[3rd] row until there are 51[55] sts. Cont without shaping until sleeve measures 5[6]cm (2[2¼]in) from beg, ending with a P row.
Shape top
Cast off 2 sts at beg of next 2 rows. Dec one st at each end of next and foll 4 alt rows, ending with a P row. Cast off 2 sts at beg of next 12[14] rows. Cast off rem 13 sts.

Neckband
Join shoulder seams. Using No.11 needles, A and with RS of work facing, K across sts of left back neck, K up 16 sts down left front neck, K across front neck sts, K up 16 sts up right front neck, then K across sts of right back neck. 61[65] sts.
Next row K2, *P1, K1, rep from * to last st, K1.
Next row K3, *P1, K1, rep from * to last 2 sts, K2.
Rep these 2 rows until neckband measures 2.5cm (1in) from beg. Cast off loosely in rib.

To make up
Press under a damp cloth with a warm iron. Set in sleeves. Join side and sleeve seams. Press seams. Sew 2 buttons to back neck opening and make loops to correspond.

Christening robe

Size
To fit 45.5/51cm (18/20in) chest
Length to shoulder, 81.5cm (32in)
Sleeve seam, 18cm (7in) including cuff

Tension
24 sts and 12 rows to 10cm (3.9in) over tr worked on No.3.00 (ISR) hook

Materials
11 x 20grm balls Sirdar Wash 'N' Wear Baby 3 ply
One No.2.50 (ISR) crochet hook
One No.3.00 (ISR) crochet hook
6 small buttons
Narrow ribbon

Skirt first motif
Using No.2.50 (ISR) hook make 7ch. Join with a ss into first ch to form a circle.
1st round 1ch to count as first dc, 11dc into circle. Join with a ss into first ch. 12dc.
2nd round 6ch to count as first tr and 3ch, (miss 1dc, 1tr into next dc, 3ch) 5 times, miss 1dc. Join with a ss into 3rd of 6ch.
3rd round Into each ch sp work (1dc, 2tr, 2dtr, 2tr, 1dc). Join with a ss into first dc.
4th round 8ch to count as first tr and 5ch, (take ch behind next petal and work 1tr around bar of tr 2 rounds below, 5ch) 5 times. Join with a ss into 3rd of 8ch.
5th round Into each ch sp work (1dc, 3tr, 4dtr, 3tr, 1dc). Join with a ss into first dc.
Rep 4th and 5th rounds once more.
8th round (3ch, ss into 3rd ch from hook, 3ch – picot worked –, miss 2 sts, 1dc into next st) to end. Join with a ss into base of first loop. 24 picots.
9th round Ss to centre of first loop, *5ch, 1dc into next loop – corner worked –, (picot, 1dc into next loop) 5 times, rep from * 3 times more, working last dc into base of 5ch.
10th round *3ch, 7tr into same loop, 3ch, 1dc into same loop, (picot, 1dc into next loop), 5 times, ss into next loop, rep from * 3 times more, working last dc into base of 3ch.
11th round Ss to top of 3ch, *picot, 1dc into 4th tr, picot, 1dc into top of 3ch, work 5 picots to top of 3ch at next corner, rep from * 3 times more. Join with a ss into base of first picot.
12th round Ss to centre of first loop, *5ch, 1dc into next picot, work 6 picots to next corner, rep from * 3 times more. Join with a ss into base of 5ch.
13th round *3ch, 7tr into same loop, 3ch, 1dc into same loop, work 6 picots to next corner, ss into corner sp, rep from * 3

Delicate and white for a cherished newborn baby: a beautiful Christening robe to crochet, trimmed with rose motifs (left); cute trouser suit in lacy crochet (centre); and behind, a gossamer-light Shetland lace shawl.

times more. Join with a ss into base of 3ch.
14th round As 11th, but work 6 picots between corners.
15th round Ss into 3ch loop of first picot, *9ch, 1dc into next 3ch loop (5ch, 1dc into next 3ch loop) 7 times, rep from * 3 times more, working last dc into first ss. Fasten off.

Second motif
Work as given for first motif until 14th round has been completed.
15th round Ss into 3ch loop of first picot, 4ch, 1dc into 9ch loop on first motif, 4ch, 1dc into next 3ch loop on second motif (2ch, 1dc into next 5ch loop on first motif, 2ch, 1dc into next 3ch loop on second motif) 7 times, 4ch, 1dc into 9ch loop on first motif, 4ch, 1dc into next 3ch loop on second motif, complete as given for 15th round of first motif.
Make a total of 24 motifs in all, joining into a tube that is 6 motifs round and 4 motifs deep.

Bodice
Using No.2.50 (ISR) hook and with RS of work facing, rejoin yarn to any corner join of motifs, 1dc into this 9ch loop, *(5ch, 1dc into next 5ch loop) 7 times, (5ch, 1dc into next 9ch loop) twice, rep from * across all 6 motifs, ending with 5ch, 1dc into last 9ch loop. Turn. 52 loops.
Next row *4ch, 1dc into next 5ch loop, rep from * to end. Turn.
Next row *3ch, 1dc into next 4ch loop, rep from * to end. Turn.
Next row *2ch, 1dc into next 3ch loop, rep from * to end. Turn.
Change to No.3.00 (ISR) hook.
Next row 3ch to count as first tr, 2tr into each 2ch loop to end. Turn.
Next row (ribbon slotting row) 4ch, miss first 2tr, 1tr into next tr, *1ch, miss 1tr, 1tr into next tr, rep from *, ending with last tr into 3rd of 3ch. Turn.
Next row 3ch, 2tr into each ch sp to end. Turn. 105tr.

Right back
Next row 3ch, miss first tr, 1tr into each of next 22tr, turn.
Complete this side first for right back.
Next row 3ch, miss first tr, 1tr into each tr, ending with last tr into 3rd of 3ch. Turn.
Rep last row 7 times more.
Next row Ss into each of first 7tr, 3ch, 1tr into each tr to end. Fasten off.

Front
Return to where work was left, miss next 6 sts for underarm, rejoin yarn to next st, 3ch, 1tr into each of next 46tr, turn.
Work 5 rows in tr without shaping.

Shape neck
Next row 3ch, miss first tr, 1tr into each of next 11tr, turn.
Work 2 rows in tr without shaping.
Next row 3ch, miss first tr, 1tr into each of next 5tr. Fasten off.
Return to where work was left at neck, miss centre 23 sts, rejoin yarn to next st, 3ch, work in tr to end. Complete to match first side.

Left back
Return to where work was left, miss next 6 sts for underarm, rejoin yarn to next st, 3ch, work in tr to end. Complete to match right back, reversing shaping at shoulder. Fasten off.

Sleeves
Join shoulder seams. Using No.2.50 (ISR) hook and with RS of work facing, rejoin yarn to first row end on front armhole edge, 1dc into this row end, *3ch, 1dc into next row end, 3ch, 1dc into same row end, rep from * all round armhole, working only into row ends, turn.
Next row *3ch, 1dc into next 3ch loop, rep from * to end. Turn.
Rep last row 25 times more.
Next row 2ch to count as first htr, *1htr into next 3ch loop, rep from * to end. Turn.
Next row 2ch, miss first htr, 1htr into each htr, ending with last htr into 2nd of 2ch. Turn.
Next row (ribbon slotting row) 4ch, miss first 2htr, 1tr into next htr, *1ch, miss 1htr, 1tr into next htr, rep from * to end, working last tr into 2nd of 2ch. Turn.
Next row 3ch, 1dc into first tr, *3ch, 1dc into next tr, rep from * to end. Turn.
Next row *3ch, 1dc into next 3ch loop, rep from * to end. Turn.
Rep last row twice more.
Next row (picot row) Into each 3ch loop work (2dc, 3ch, ss into last dc worked, 1dc). Fasten off. Make second sleeve in the same way, starting with first row end of back armhole edge.

Neck frill
Using No.2.50 (ISR) hook and with RS of work facing, rejoin yarn to corner of neck edge on left back, 1dc into same place, *3ch, miss one st, 1dc into next st, rep from * to shoulder seam, 3ch and 1dc into each row end down neck edge, work as given for back along front neck, 3ch and 1dc into each row end up neck edge and work as given for back along right back neck to corner. Turn.
Next row *3ch, 1dc into next 3ch loop, rep from * to end. Turn.
Rep last row twice more. Fasten off.

To make up
Join back seam to one row below ribbon slotting row.
Back and neck edging Using No.2.50 (ISR) hook and with RS of work facing, rejoin yarn to row end on left back edge, 2dc into each row end to top of neck frill, work picot row as given for sleeves along 3ch loops of neck frill, then work 2dc into each row end down right back edge. Join with a ss into first dc of left back edge.
Next row Work (3ch, miss 2dc, 1dc into each of next 3dc) 5 times up left back edge, 3ch, miss 2dc, 1dc into next dc. Fasten off. 6 button loops made.
Lower edging Using No.2.50 (ISR) hook and with RS of work facing, join yarn to any ch loop and into every loop work (3dc,

3ch, ss into last dc worked, 2dc). Join with a ss into first dc. Fasten off.
Press under a damp cloth with a warm iron, blocking out motifs so that they lie flat. Join sleeves seams, placing first row ends to shaped underarm section. Sew on buttons to correspond with button loops. Thread ribbon through slots at underarm, sleeves and neck.

Shetland lace shawl

Size
144cm (56½in) x 104cm (41in)
Tension
Each motif worked on No.3.50 (ISR) hook measures 15cm (6in) across diameter
Materials
6 x 25grm balls Templetons H & O Shetland Lace
One No.3.50 (ISR) crochet hook

1st strip – 1st motif
Using No.3.50 (ISR) hook make 6ch. Join with a ss into first ch to form circle.
1st round 2ch, 11dc into circle. Join with a ss into 2nd of 2ch. 12 sts.
2nd round 3ch, 1tr into same place as ss, 2tr into each dc to end. Join with a ss into 3rd of 3ch. 24 sts.
3rd round 6ch, *miss 1tr, 1dc into next tr, 5ch, rep from * 11 times more, miss 1tr. Join with a ss into first of 6ch.
4th round Ss to centre of first loop, *3ch, (3tr, 2ch, 3tr) – called shell – into next loop, 3ch, 1dc into next loop, rep from * to end, working last dc into base of first 3ch.
5th round *4ch, shell into 2ch sp of next shell, 4ch, 1dc into next dc, rep from * to end.
6th round As 5th round, working 5ch instead of 4ch.
7th round As 5th round, working 6ch instead of 4ch and ending with a ss into dc at end of last round. Fasten off.
2nd motif
Work first 6 rounds as given for 1st motif.
7th round 6ch, 3tr into 2ch sp of shell, 1ch, insert hook into 2ch sp of a shell on 1st motif and work a ss, 1ch, 3tr into same sp on 2nd motif, 3ch, ss into 6ch loop on 1st motif, 3ch, 1dc into next dc on 2nd motif, 3ch, ss into next 6ch loop on 1st motif, 3ch, 3tr into 2ch sp of next shell on 2nd motif, 1ch, ss into 2ch sp of shell on 1st motif, 1ch, 3tr into same 2ch sp on 2nd motif, patt to end of 2nd motif. Fasten off.
Make 6 more motifs (8 in all), joining in the same way.

2nd strip – 9th motif
Work first 6 rounds as given for 1st motif.
7th round 3ch, 3tr into 2ch sp of shell, 1ch, ss into 2ch sp of shell at side of 1st motif, *1ch, 3tr into same 2ch sp on 9th

motif, 3ch, ss into 6ch loop on 1st motif, 3ch, 1dc into dc on 9th motif, 3ch, ss into next 6ch loop on 1st motif, 3ch, 3tr into next 2ch sp on 9th motif, 1ch, *, ss into join of 1st and 2nd motifs, rep from * to * but working into 2nd motif instead of 1st, ss into next 2ch sp on 2nd motif, 1ch, 3tr into same sp on 9th motif, patt to end of 9th motif. Fasten off.

10th motif
Work first 6 rounds as given for 1st motif.
7th round 3ch, 3tr into 2ch sp of shell, 1ch, ss into 4th 2ch sp of 9th motif, *1ch, 3tr into same sp on 10th motif, 3ch, ss into 6ch loop on 9th motif, 3ch, 1dc into dc on 10th motif, 3ch, ss into next 6ch loop on 9th motif, 3ch, 3tr into next 2ch sp on 10th motif, 1ch, *, ss into join of 9th and 2nd motifs, rep from * to * joining to 2nd motif, ss into join of 2nd and 3rd motifs, rep from * to * joining to 3rd motif, ss into 2ch sp at side of 3rd motif, patt to end of 10th motif. Fasten off.
Cont in this way, working 5 more motifs in this strip and joining as before.
Work strips of 6, 5, 4, 3, 2 and 1 motifs to form a triangular shape. Turn work and work 7 motifs, joining to other side of first strip of 8. Then work strips of 6, 5, 4, 3, 2 and 1 motifs, joining as before.

To make up
Edging Using No.3.50 (ISR) hook and with RS of work facing, join yarn to dc at centre of lower edge of 1st motif, *8ch, 1dc into 2ch sp of shell, (4ch, 1dc) 3 times into same sp, 8ch, 1dc into next dc, 8ch, 1dc into 2ch sp before join, 4ch, (1dc, 4ch, 1dc) into join, 4ch, 1dc into next 2ch sp after join, 8ch, 1dc into next dc, rep from * all round. Join with a ss into place where yarn was joined. Fasten off.
Pin out to size. Press under a damp cloth with a warm iron.

Crochet trouser suit

Sizes
To fit 45.5[51]cm (18[20]in) chest
Top length to shoulder, 23[25.5]cm (9[10]in)
Sleeve seam, 7.5cm (3in)
Trousers waist to crutch, 15[18]cm (6[7]in)
Inside leg seam, 18[20.5]cm (7[8]in)
The figures in brackets [ ] refer to the 51cm (20in) size only
Tension
25 sts and 18 rows to 10cm (3.9in) over htr worked on No.3.00 (ISR) hook
Materials
6 x 20grm balls Sirdar Wash 'N' Wear Baby 3 ply

One No.3.00 (ISR) crochet hook
One No.3.50 (ISR) crochet hook
3 small buttons
1.80 metres (2 yards) narrow ribbon

Top front bodice
Using No.3.00 (ISR) hook make 49[55]ch.
Base row Into 3rd ch from hook work 1htr, 1htr into each ch to end. Turn. 48[54] htr.
1st row 2ch to count as first htr, miss first htr, 1htr into each htr to end, finishing with last htr into 2nd of 2ch. Turn.
Rep last row twice more.
Shape armholes
Next row Ss into 4th [5th] htr, 2ch, 1htr into each htr to last 3[4] sts, turn. 42[46] htr.
Work 9[11] rows in htr on these sts.
Shape neck and shoulders
Next row 2ch, miss first htr, 1htr into each of next 14[15] htr, turn.
Complete this side first.
Next row 2ch, miss first htr, leaving last loop of each on hook work 1htr into each of next 2htr, yrh and draw through all loops on hook – called dec 1htr –, 1htr into each htr to end. Turn.
Next row Ss into 5th[6th] htr, 2ch, 1htr into each htr to last st, miss last st, turn.
Next row 2ch, miss first htr, dec 1htr, work to last 4 sts. Fasten off.
Return to where work was left, miss 12[14] sts for centre front neck, rejoin yarn to next st, 2ch, patt to end. Complete to match first side, reversing shaping.

Top right back bodice
Using No.3.00 (ISR) hook make 26[29] ch.
Base row Into 3rd ch from hook work 1htr, 1htr into each ch to end. Turn. 25[28] htr.
Work 3 rows in htr as given for front bodice.
Shape armhole
Next row Ss into 4th[5th] htr, 2ch, work to end. Turn. 22[24] htr.
Cont in htr without shaping until work measures same as front to shoulder, ending at armhole edge.
Shape shoulder
Next row Ss into 5th[6th] htr, 2ch, work to end. Turn.
Next row Work to last 4[5] sts, turn.
Next row Ss into 5th[6th] htr, 2ch, work to end. Fasten off.

Top left back bodice
Work as given for right back bodice, reversing shaping.

Top skirt
Join bodice side seams. With RS of work facing, rejoin yarn to lower edge of right back bodice and cont across bodice as foll:
1st row 4ch to count as first dtr, 3dtr into st at base of ch, *miss 2 sts, 7dtr into next st, rep from * to last 3 sts, miss 2 sts, 4dtr into last st. Turn.
2nd row 1ch, 1dc into top of first dtr, *3ch, 1tr into sp between groups, 3ch, 1dc

into centre dtr of next group, rep from *, ending with 3ch, 1tr into sp, 3ch, 1dc into top of 4ch. Turn.

3rd row 4ch, 3dtr into first dc, *7dtr into next dc, rep from *, ending with 4dtr into last dc. Turn.

Rep last 2 rows 6[7] times more or until work is required length. Fasten off.

Sleeves

Using No.3.00 (ISR) hook make 36[39] ch. and beg at top.

Base row Into 4th ch from hook work 1tr, 1tr into each ch to end. Turn. 34[37] tr.

Work 1st – 3rd patt rows as given for skirt, then rep 2nd and 3rd rows twice more and 2nd row again.

Next row 1ch, 1dc into first st, 2dc into each 3ch sp. Turn.

Next row 1ch, 1dc into each dc to end. Turn.

Next row (ribbon slotting row) 4ch to count as first tr and ch, miss first 2dc, *1tr into next dc, 1ch, miss 1dc, rep from *, ending with 1tr into last dc. Turn.

Next row 1ch, 1dc into first tr, 2dc into each 1ch sp to end.
Fasten off.

To make up

Press under a damp cloth with a warm iron. Join shoulder seams. Set in sleeves, placing base row into straight section of armhole and first 3 rows of patt to shaped underarm section. Join rem sleeve seam.

Neck edging Using No.3.00 (ISR) hook and with RS of work facing, beg at lower edge of left back opening and work 1 row of dc up left back, round neck and down right back. Turn. Work a second row of dc, dec one st at corners of neck and shoulders and working 2dc into corners at centre back. Fasten off.

Make 3 worked buttonholes on right back. Sew on buttons to correspond. Thread ribbon through slots on sleeves and tie in a bow.

Trousers

Using No.3.50 (ISR) hook make 92[104] ch for waist edge. Join with a ss into first ch to form a circle.

1st round 1ch to count as first dc, miss first ch, 1dc into each ch to end. Join with a ss into first ch.

Work 4 more rounds in dc. Change to No.3.00 (ISR) hook. Commence patt.

1st round 4ch to count as first dtr, 4dtr into dc at base of ch, miss 3dc, *5dtr into next dc, miss 3dc, rep from * all round. Join with a ss into 4th of 4ch. 23[25] groups.

2nd round Ss into sp under ss just made, 5ch to count as first tr and 2ch, *1dc into centre dtr of next group, 2ch, 1tr into next sp between groups, 2ch, rep from * all round. Join with a ss into 3rd of 5ch.

3rd round Ss into first dc, 4ch, 4dtr into same dc, *5dtr into next dc, rep from * all round. Join with a ss into 4th of 4ch.
Rep 2nd and 3rd rounds 4[5] times more,

then work 2nd round again.

Next round As 3rd round, but work 7dtr into each dc.

Next round As 2nd round, but work 3ch instead of 2ch.

Divide for legs

Next round Patt across first 7[8] groups, miss next 11[12] dc, 7dtr into next dc, patt to end. Join with a ss into 4th of 4ch. 12[13] groups.

Cont in rounds of patt as before, working 3ch instead of 2ch and 7dtr on each group round, until leg measures 18[20.5]cm *(7[8]in)* from division, ending with a 3rd round. Fasten off.

Return to where work was left, rejoin yarn to 7th[8th] group of first leg, 4ch, 6dtr into same dc, patt to end of round. Join with a ss into 4th of 4ch. 12[13] groups. Complete as given for first leg. Fasten off.

To make up

Press as given for top. If necessary stitch up small space left at crutch division and run shirring elastic through waist edge.

Crochet jacket with hood

Photograph overleaf

Sizes

To fit 46cm *(18in)* chest
Length to shoulder, 28cm *(11in)*
Sleeve seam, 18cm *(7in)*

Tension

9 groups and 16 rows to 10cm *(3.9in)* over patt worked on No.4.00 (ISR) hook

Materials

10 x 25grm balls Lee Target Superwash Wool Double Knitting
One No.4.00 (ISR) crochet hook
5 buttons
Oddments of colours, A, B and C, for flowers

Jacket back and fronts

Using No.4.00 (ISR) hook make 98ch and work in one piece to underarm.

1st row Into 3rd ch from hook work 1dc, 1dc into each ch to end. Turn. 97dc.

2nd row 1ch, 1htr into first dc (edge st), *miss 1dc, (1dc and 1htr) into next dc – called 1gr –, rep from * to last 2dc, miss 1dc, 1dc into turning ch. Turn. 48gr.

3rd row 1ch, 1htr into first dc (edge st), *1gr into next dc, rep from * to end, 1dc into turning ch. Turn.

Rep 3rd row until work measures 16cm *(6¼in)* from beg.

Divide for armholes

1st row 1ch, 1htr into first dc (edge st), 1gr into each of next 10dc, 1dc into next dc, turn. Cont on these 11gr for right front.

2nd row 1ch, miss first dc (edge st), 1gr into next dc, patt to end. Turn. 10gr.

3rd row 1ch, 1htr into first dc (edge st), 1gr into each dc to end, 1dc into turning ch. Turn. 10gr.

4th row As 2nd. 9gr.

Cont without shaping until armhole measures 7cm *(2¾in)* from beg, ending at armhole edge.

Shape neck

Next row 1ch, 1htr into first dc, 1gr into each of next 6dc, 1dc into next dc, turn. 7gr.

Next row 1ch, miss first dc, 1gr into each dc to end. Turn. 6gr.

Next row Patt to end. Turn.

Rep last 2 rows once more. 5gr. Cont without shaping until armhole measures 12cm *(4¾in)* from beg, ending at neck edge.

Shape shoulder

Next row 1ch, 1htr into first dc, 1gr into each of next 2dc, ss into next dc. Fasten off.
Return to where work was left, rejoin yarn to next dc, 1ch, 1gr into each of next 22dc, 1dc into next dc, turn.
Cont on these 22gr for back.

Next row 1ch, 1gr into each dc to end, 1dc into turning ch. Turn.

Rep last row 3 times more. 18gr. Cont without shaping until armholes measure same as front to shoulder.

Shape shoulders

Next row Ss over first 2gr, 1ch, 1gr into each dc to last 2gr, ss into next dc. Fasten off.
Return to where work was left, rejoin yarn to next dc, 1ch, 1gr into each dc to end, 1dc into turning ch. Turn. 11gr. Complete left front to match right front.

Sleeves

Using No.4.00 (ISR) hook make 30ch.
Work 1st–3rd rows as given for back and fronts. 14gr. Rep 3rd row 3 times more.

7th row Patt to end, finishing with 1gr into turning ch. Turn.

8th row 1ch, 1gr into first dc, patt to end, finishing with 1gr into turning ch. Turn.

9th row 1ch, 1gr into first dc, patt to end, finishing with 1gr into last dc, 1dc into turning ch. Turn.

10th row 1ch, 1htr into first dc (edge st), patt to end, finishing with 1gr into last dc, 1dc into turning ch. Turn.

11th row 1ch, 1htr into first dc (edge st), patt to end. Turn. 16gr.

12th row Patt to end. Turn.

Rep last 6 rows twice more. 20gr. Cont without shaping until sleeve measures 18cm *(7in)* from beg.

Shape top

Next row 1ch, miss first dc (edge st), 1gr into next dc, patt to end. Turn.

Rep last row 5 times more. Fasten off. 14gr.

Hood

Using No.4.00 (ISR) hook make 64ch.
Work 1st-3rd rows as given for back and fronts. 31gr. Rep 3rd row 5 times more.

9th row 1ch, 1htr into first dc (edge st), 1gr into each of next 13dc, 2gr into next dc, 1gr into next dc, 2gr into next dc, patt to end. Turn. 33gr.

Patt 5 rows.

15th row 1ch, 1htr into first dc (edge st), 1gr into each of next 14dc, 2gr into next dc, 1gr into next dc, 2gr into next dc, patt to end. Turn. 35gr.
Cont without shaping until work measures 18cm *(7in)* from beg.
Next row 1ch, 1htr into first dc (edge st), 1gr into each of next 14dc, 1dc into next dc, turn.
Cont on these 15gr for 2cm *(¾in)*. Fasten off.
Return to where work was left, miss next 4dc, rejoin yarn to next dc, 1ch, 1htr into same dc, patt to end. Turn. Complete to match other side.

To make up
Do not press. Join shoulder seams. Join sleeve seams. Set in sleeves. Join two pieces at top of hood, then join side edges of this part to section which was left in centre.

Edging Using No.4.00 (ISR) hook and with RS of work facing, rejoin yarn at left front neck edge and work 1 row dc down left front, round lower edge and up right front. Break off yarn. Rejoin yarn at left front neck edge and work a 2nd row of dc, making 5 evenly spaced buttonholes up right front edge by working 2ch and missing 2dc for each. Do not break off yarn, but work a row of crab st all round.
Round sleeve and face edges of hood work 1 row dc and one row crab st.
Neck edging Work an odd number of dc round neck edge. Turn.
Next row 4ch to count as first tr and ch,

Below right : Crochet jacket for a baby with hood attached, decorated with coloured flower motifs. Below left : Baby bag with zip fastener in four colour stripes and a drawstring at the hem to keep small feet nice and warm.

miss 1dc, *1tr into next dc, 1ch, miss 1dc, rep from * ending with 1tr into last dc. Fasten off.
Turn 4cm *(1½in)* of face edge of hood to RS, then work edging as given for neck round neck edge of hood. Join hood to neck edge. Press seams under a damp cloth with a warm iron. Sew on buttons. Using yarn double make a twisted cord approx 110cm *(47½in)* long and thread through holes at neck.
Flower motifs (make 2) Using No.4.00 (ISR) hook and A, make 4ch. Join with a ss into first ch to form a circle.
Next round 1ch, 7dc into circle. Join with a ss into first ch. Break off A. Join in B.
Next round 1ch, ss into first dc, *3tr into next dc, 1dc into next dc, rep from * twice more, 3tr into next dc. Join with a ss into first ch. Fasten off.
Stem Join C to 1dc on last round, 11ch, into 10th and foll 4ch work 1dc and 10ch, into 9th and foll 4ch work 1dc, miss 3ch, 1dc into each of next 6ch back to flower. Fasten off.

Baby bag with zip

Sizes
To fit approx 6 months–1 year
Length, 71cm *(28in)*
Sleeve seam, 16cm *(6¼in)*
Tension
24 sts and 30 rows to 10cm *(3.9in)* over st st worked on No.9 needles
Materials
7 x 25grm balls Lee Target Motoravia Double Knitting in main shade, A
5 balls of contrast colour, B
2 balls of contrast colour, C
2 balls of contrast colour, D
One pair No.9 needles
One No.3.00 (ISR) crochet hook
40cm *(16in)* zip fastener
Narrow elastic for sleeves

Back
Using No.9 needles and B, cast on 108 sts. Beg with a K row, cont in st st and stripe sequence of 4 rows B, 2 rows C, 6 rows A and 2 rows D throughout. Dec one st at each end of 17th and every foll 16th row until 88 sts rem. Cont without shaping until 180 rows have been completed, ending with 6th row of an A stripe.
Shape armholes
Next row K1, sl 1, K2 tog, psso, K to last 4 sts, K3 tog, K1.
Next row P to end.
Rep last 2 rows 6 times more. 60 sts. Cont without shaping until 38 rows have been completed from beg of armholes, ending with 2nd row of an A stripe.
Shape shoulders and neck
Next row Cast off 5, K20, turn and leave

rem sts on holder.
Complete this side first. Cast off at beg of next and every row 5 sts 4 times.
With RS of work facing, rejoin A to sts on holder, cast off 10, K to end. Cast off at beg of next and every row 5 sts 5 times.

Front
Work 82 rows as given for back, ending with 6th row of an A stripe. 98 sts.
Divide for opening
Next row K49, turn and leave rem sts on holder.
Complete this side first. Cont to dec at side edge as before on every 16th row until 44 sts rem. Cont without shaping until work matches back to underarm, ending at side edge.
Shape armhole
Next row K1, sl 1, K2 tog, psso, K to end.
Next row P to end.
Rep last 2 rows 6 times more. 30 sts. Work 9 more rows, ending at front edge.
Shape neck
Cast off at beg of next and foll alt rows 5 sts once, 3 sts once, 2 sts twice and one st 3 times. 15 sts. Work 2 rows, ending at armhole edge.
Shape shoulder
Cast off at beg of next and foll alt rows 5 sts 3 times.
With RS of work facing, rejoin yarn to rem sts and K to end. Complete to match first side, reversing shaping.

Sleeves
Using No.9 needles and B, cast on 54 sts.
Beg with a K row, work 54 rows st st in stripe sequence as given for back, ending with 6th row of an A stripe.
Shape top
Next row K1, sl 1, K1, psso, K to last 3 sts, K2 tog, K1.
Next row P to end.
Rep last 2 rows 6 times more. Cast off rem 40 sts.

To make up
Press under a damp cloth with a warm iron. Join shoulder seams. Set in sleeves. Join side and sleeve seams, leaving 4cm (1½in) open at lower edge of each side seam. Turn 2cm (¾in) hem to WS at lower and sleeve edges and sl st in position. Using No.3.00 (ISR) hook, A and with RS of work facing, work 2 rows dc along each side of front opening.
Neck edging Using No.3.00 (ISR) hook, A and with RS of work facing, work an odd number of dc round neck edge. Turn.
Next row 4ch to count as first tr and ch, miss 1dc, *1tr into next dc, 1ch, miss 1dc, rep from * ending with 1tr into last dc. Fasten off.
Sew in zip. Press all seams. Using 3 strands of A, make a twisted cord 120cm (47½in) long and thread through holes at neck. Make 2 twisted cords 150cm (60in) long and thread one through back and one through front of hem at lower edge. Thread elastic through hem of sleeves.

Rompers with crochet edging

Above : Knitted rompers keep little chests warm and allow plenty of freedom of movement. They're trimmed with crochet edging.

Sizes
To fit 45.5[51]cm (18[20]in) chest
Length to shoulder, 40[43]cm (15¾[17¼]in)
The figures in brackets [ ] refer to the 51cm (20in) size only
Tension
28 sts and 40 rows to 10cm (3.9in) over st st worked on No.10 needles
Materials
5[7] x 70 metre (77yd) balls Robin Crochet Courtelle
One pair No.10 needles
One No.2.50 (ISR) crochet hook
2 press fasteners

Back
Using No.10 needles cast on 28[32] sts for leg.
1st row *P2, K2, rep from * to end.
Rep last row 23 times more. Keeping rib correct, inc one st at beg of next and foll 2 alt rows, then rib 1 row. 31[35] sts. Break off yarn. Leave sts on holder
Using No.10 needles cast on 28[32] sts.
1st row *K2, P2, rep from * to end.
Rep last row 23 times more. Keeping rib correct, inc one st at end of next and foll 2 alt rows, then rib 1 row.
Next row (RS)Rib to end, turn and cast on 4 sts, turn and rib across sts of first leg. 66[74] sts.
Cont without shaping until work measures 27[29]cm (10¾[11½]in) from beg, ending with a WS row.

Shape armholes
Cast off 2 sts at beg of next 4 rows. Dec one st at each end of next and foll 3[4] alt rows, then at each end of every foll 4th row 4 times in all, ending with a dec row. 42[48] sts.
Shape neck
Next row Rib 15[17], cast off 12[14] sts, rib to end.
Cont on last 15[17] sts. Rib 1 row. Cast off 2 sts at beg of next row, then dec one st at neck edge on foll 3 alt rows. 10[12] sts. Cont without shaping until armhole measures 14[15]cm (5½[6]in) from beg. Cast off.
With RS of work facing, rejoin yarn to rem sts. Complete to match first side, reversing shaping.

Front
Work as given for back, but cont until armhole measures 16[17]cm (6¼[6¾]in) after completion of neck shaping.

To make up
Do not press. Join side, leg and crutch seams. Turn 1.5cm (½in) hem to WS on each leg and sl st in position.
Edging Using No.2.50 (ISR) hook and with RS of work facing, join yarn to top of one side seam and work in dc round top edges. Join with a ss into first dc.
Next round 1ch, *1dc into each of next 3dc, 3ch, 1dc into last dc worked, rep from * all round. Join with a ss into first ch. Fasten off.
Sew a press fastener to each strap at shoulder.

Short-sleeved jersey & pants

Sizes
To fit 46[51]cm (18[20]in) chest
Jersey length to shoulder, 26[29]cm (10¼[11½]in)
Sleeve seam, 5cm (2in)
Pants depth at side, 22[25]cm (8¾[9¾]in)
The figures in brackets [ ] refer to the 51cm (20in) size only

Tension
26 sts and 48 rows to 10cm (3.9in) over patt worked on No.8 needles

Materials
6[7] x 20grm balls Robin Columbine Crepe Double Knitting in main shade, A
4[5] balls of contrast colour, B
One pair No.8 needles
One pair No.10 needles
One No.3.00 (ISR) crochet hook
6 small buttons
Waist length of elastic

Jersey back
Using No.10 needles and A, cast on 61[69] sts.
1st row K1, *P1, K1, rep from * to end.
2nd row P1, *K1, P1, rep from * to end.
Rep these 2 rows until work measures 3cm (1¼in) from beg, ending with a 2nd row. Change to No.8 needles. Join in B. Commence patt.
1st row (RS) Using B, sl 1, *K3, sl 1, rep from * to end.
2nd row Using B, sl 1, *ybk, K3, yfwd, sl 1, rep from * to end.
3rd row Using A, K2, *sl 1, K3, rep from * to last 3 sts, sl 1, K2.
4th row Using A, K2, *yfwd, sl 1, ybk, K3, rep from * to last 3 sts, yfwd, sl 1, ybk, K2.
These 4 rows form patt and are rep throughout. Cont in patt until work measures 14[16]cm (5½[6¼]in) from beg, ending with a WS row.
Shape armholes
Cast off at beg of next and every row 3 sts twice, 2 sts twice and one st 2[4] times. 49[55] sts. **. Cont without shaping until armholes measure 12[13]cm (4¾[5]in) from beg, ending with a WS row.
Shape neck and shoulders
Next row Cast off 3, patt 18[21], turn and leave rem sts on holder.
Cast off at beg of next and every row *3 sts once and 3[4] sts once, rep from * twice more.
With RS of work facing, sl first 7 sts on holder for back neck, rejoin yarn to next st and patt to end. Complete to match first side, reversing shaping.

Stripes both ways for a short-sleeved jersey and pants (far left) and a zip-fronted playsuit with long legs (left).

Neckband
Using No.10 needles, A and with RS of work facing, K up 11 sts down right back neck, K across back neck sts on holder and K up 11 sts up left back neck. 29 sts. Beg with a 2nd row, work 6 rows rib. Cast off in rib.

Jersey front
Work as given for back to **. Cont without shaping until armholes measure 7[8]cm (2¾[3¼]in) from beg, ending with a WS row.
Shape neck
Next row Patt 22[25], turn and leave rem sts on holder.
Complete this side first. Cast off at beg of next and foll alt rows 3 sts once, 2 sts once and one st 5 times. 12[15] sts. Cont without shaping until armhole matches back to shoulder, ending at armhole edge.
Shape shoulder
Cast off at beg of next and foll alt rows 3 sts once and 3[4] sts 3 times.
With RS of work facing, sl first 5 sts on holder for front neck, rejoin yarn to next st and patt to end. Complete to match first side, reversing shaping.
Neckband
Using No.10 needles, A and with RS of work facing, K up 19 sts down left front neck, K across front neck sts on holder and K up 19 sts up right front neck. 43 sts. Complete as given for back neckband.

Sleeves
Using No.10 needles and A, cast on 49[53] sts. Work 3cm (1¼in) rib as given for back, ending with a 2nd row and inc 4 sts evenly across last row. 53[57] sts. Change to No.8 needles. Cont in patt as given for back until sleeve measures approx 5cm (2in) from beg, ending with same patt row as back and front at underarm.
Shape top
Cast off at beg of next and every row 2 sts twice, one st 32[36] times, 2 sts 4 times and 9 sts once.

To make up
Press under a damp cloth with a cool iron. Join shoulder seams for 1cm (½in) from armhole edge. Set in sleeves. Join side and sleeve seams. Using No.3.00 (ISR) hook and A, work a row of dc round shoulder openings, making 3 button loops on each front shoulder. Press seams. Sew on buttons.

Pants left half
Using No.10 needles and A, cast on 65[73] sts. Work 3cm (1¼in) rib as given for jersey, ending with a 2nd row. Change to No.8 needles. Cont in patt as given for jersey, inc one st at each end of 3rd and every foll 4th row until there are 75[83] sts. Cont without shaping until work measures 8cm (3¼in) from beg, ending with a WS row.
Shape crutch
Cast off at beg of next and every row 3 sts once, one st once, 2 sts once and one st 4 times. 65[73] sts. Cont without shaping until work measures 20[23]cm (7¾[9]in) from beg, ending with a WS row. Break off B. Change to No.10 needles. Using A, work 4cm (1½in) rib. Cast off in rib.

Pants right half
Work to match left half, reversing shaping at crutch.

To make up
Press as given for jersey. Join back and front seams. Join leg seams. Fold waistband in half to inside and sl st in position. Press seams. Thread elastic through waist.

Zip-fronted playsuit

Sizes
To fit 51[56]cm (20[22]in) chest
Length from back neck to crutch, 38[41]cm (15[16¼]in)
Inside leg seam, 26[29]cm (10¼[11½]in)
Sleeve seam, 6cm (2¼in)
The figures in brackets [ ] refer to the 56cm (22in) size only

Tension
26 sts and 32 rows to 10cm (3.9in) over st st worked on No.9 needles

Materials
7[9] x 20grm balls Robin Columbine Crepe Double Knitting in main shade, A
5[6] balls of contrast colour, B
One pair No.9 needles
One pair No.11 needles
One No.3.00 (ISR) crochet hook
30[35]cm (12[14]in) zip fastener

Right leg
Using No.11 needles and B, cast on 74[80] sts. Work 2cm (¾in) g st. Change to No.9 needles. Join in A. Beg with a K row, cont in st st, working in stripe sequence of 4 rows A and 2 rows B throughout, until work measures 13[14]cm (5[5½]in) from beg, ending with a P row. Inc one st at each end of next and every foll 16th[18th] row until there are 80[86] sts. Cont without shaping until work measures 26[29]cm (10¼[11½]in) from beg, ending with a P row.
Shape crutch
Dec one st at each end of next and foll 2 alt rows, ending with a K row. **. Leave rem 74[80] sts on holder.

Left leg
Work as given for right leg to **.
Join legs
Next row P73[79], P next st tog with first st of right leg, P across right leg sts. 147[159] sts.
Cont without shaping until work measures approx 26[28]cm (10¼[11]in) from join, ending with 2nd row of a B stripe.

Divide for armholes
Next row K34[37], cast off 6, K67[73], cast off 6, K to end.
Cont on last 34[37] sts for left front. P 1 row. Cast off 2 sts at beg of next and foll alt row. Dec one st at beg of foll 2[3] alt rows. 28[30] sts. Cont without shaping until armhole measures 8[9]cm (3¼[3½]in) from beg, ending at armhole edge.
Shape neck
Next row K24[25], turn and leave rem 4[5] sts on holder.
Cast off 3 sts at beg of next row and 2 sts at beg of foll alt row. Dec one st at end of next and foll 4 alt rows, ending at armhole edge. 14[15] sts.
Shape shoulder
Cast off at beg of next and foll alt rows 5 sts twice and 4[5] sts once.
With WS of work facing, rejoin yarn to back sts and P to end. Cast off 2 sts at beg of next 4 rows. Dec one st at each end of next and foll 1[2] alt rows. 55[59] sts. Cont without shaping until armholes match front to shoulder, ending with a P row.
Shape neck and shoulders
Next row Cast off 5, K19[20], turn and leave rem sts on holder.
Complete this side first. Cast off at beg of next and every row 5 sts 3 times and 4[5] sts once.
With RS of work facing, sl first 7[9] sts on holder for back neck, rejoin yarn to next st and K to end. Cast off at beg of next and every row 5 sts 4 times and 4[5] sts once.
With WS of work facing, rejoin yarn to sts for right front and P to end. Complete to match left front, reversing shaping.

Sleeves
Using No.11 needles and B, cast on 48[52] sts. Work 2cm (¾in) g st. Change to No.9 needles. Join in A. Beg with a K row, cont in st st and stripe sequence as before, inc one st at each end of first and every foll 3rd row until there are 54[58] sts. Work 2 rows, ending with a P row.
Shape top
Cast off at beg of next and every row 3 sts twice, one st 12 times, 2 sts 14[16] times and 8 sts once.

Neckband
Join shoulder seams. Using N.11 needles, B and with RS of work facing, K up 64[70] sts evenly round neck, including sts on holders. K 12 rows g st. Cast off.

Pockets
Using No.11 needles and A, cast on 24[28] sts. Work 8[9]cm (3¼[3½]in) g st. Cast off. Make another pocket using B.

To make up
Press under a damp cloth with a cool iron. Join sleeve seams. Set in sleeves. Join leg seams. Using No.3.00 (ISR) hook and B, work 2 rows dc along each side of front opening. Sew in zip. Join rem part of front seam below zip. Sew on pockets as shown in picture. Press seams.

Toddler's coat with contrast pattern

Sizes
To fit 56cm (22in) chest
Length to shoulder, 42cm (16½in)
Sleeve seam, 18cm (7in)
Tension
28 sts and 36 rows to 10cm (3.9in) over st st worked on No.10 needles
Materials
8 x 25grm balls Patons Trident 4 ply in main shade, A
1 ball of contrast colour, B
One pair No.10 needles
One No.3.00 (ISR) crochet hook
2 buttons

Back
Using No.10 needles and A, cast on 94 sts. Beg with a K row, cont in st st until work measures 5cm (2in) from beg, ending with a K row.
Next row K to end to form hemline.
Beg with a K row, cont in st st until work measures 29cm (11½in) from hemline, ending with a P row. **.
Shape armholes
Dec one st at each end of next and foll 12 rows. 68 sts. Cont without shaping until armholes measure 13cm (5in) from beg, ending with a P row. Cast off.

Right front
Using No.10 needles and A, cast on 46 sts. Work as given for back to **.
Shape armhole
Join in B. Commence patt.
Next row K4 A, 1 B, 2 A, 3 B, 2 A, 1 B, cont in A to last 2 sts, K2 tog.
Next row P2 tog, P30 A, (1 B, 3 A) 3 times, 1 A.
Next row K3 A, 3 B, 5 A, 3 B, cont in A to last 2 sts, K2 tog.
Cont in this way, working in patt from chart and dec one st at armhole edge on next 10 rows. 33 sts. Cont without shaping until 40 rows have been completed from beg of patt, ending with a WS row.
Shape neck
Cast off 15 sts at beg of next row. 18 sts. Cont without shaping until armhole measures same as back to shoulder, ending with a P row. Cast off.

Left front
Work to match right front, reversing shaping and patt as shown.
Shape armhole
Next row K2 tog, K31 A, 1 B, 2 A, 3 B, 2 A, 1 B, 4 A.
Next row P4 A, (1 B, 3 A) twice, 1 B, cont in A to last 2 sts, P2 tog.

Right sleeve
Using No.10 needles and A, cast on 55 sts.

Join in B. Commence patt.
1st row K11 A, (1 B, 2 A, 3 B, 2 A) 5 times, 1 B, 3 A.
2nd row P (3 A, 1 B) to last 11 sts, 11 A to end.
3rd row K10 A, (3 B, 5 A) 5 times, 3 B, 2 A.
4th row P1 A, (5 B, 3 A) to last 14 sts, 5 B, 9 A.
Cont in this way, working in patt from chart and keeping 9 sts at right edge and one st at left edge of work in A throughout, until 70 rows have been completed from beg. Cast off.

Left sleeve
Work as given for right sleeve, keeping 9 sts at left edge and one st at right edge of work in A as shown.
1st row K3 A, 1 B, (2 A, 3 B, 2 A, 1 B) 5 times, 11 A.
2nd row P11 A, (1 B, 3 A) to end.

To make up
Press under a damp cloth with a warm iron. Join shoulder seams. Set in sleeves, noting that edge of work with 9 sts in A forms cuff. Join side and sleeve seams. Turn hem to WS at hemline and sl st in position. Turn 5 sts at lower edge of sleeves to WS for hem and sl st in position.
Edging Using No.3.00 (ISR) hook, A and with RS of work facing, work a row of dc up right front, round neck and down left front. Turn.
Next row (buttonhole row) Work in dc to top of right front, 3ch, miss 3dc, cont in dc to lower edge of patt, 3ch, miss 3dc, cont in dc to end. Turn.
Work 3 more rows dc. Fasten off.
Press seams. Sew on buttons.

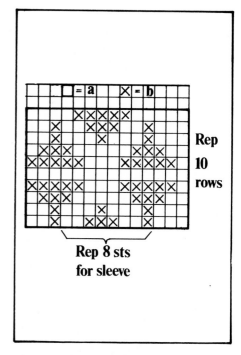

Right : Toddler's coat with contrast pattern on yoke and sleeves. Above : Chart for working pattern.

Jersey with shirt collar

Sizes

To fit 46[51]cm *(18[20]in)* chest
Length to shoulder, 27[30]cm
(10½[11¾]in)

Sleeve seam, 16[18]cm *(6¼[7]in)*
The figures in brackets [ ] refer to the 51cm
(20in) size only

Tension

24 sts and 32 rows to 10cm *(3.9in)* over st
st worked on No.9 needles

Materials

5[6] x 20grm balls Lister Easywash
Double Knitting in main shade, A
1 ball of contrast colour, B
One pair No.9 needles

One pair No.11 needles
One No.3.00 (ISR) crochet hook
10cm *(4in)* zip fastener

Back

Using No.11 needles and A, cast on 57[63]
sts.
1st row K1, *P1, K1, rep from * to end.
2nd row P1, *K1, P1, rep from * to end.
Rep these 2 rows until work measures 3cm
(1¼in) from beg, ending with a 2nd row

and inc one st in centre of last row. 58[64] sts. Change to No.9 needles. Beg with a K row cont in st st until work measures 16[18]cm *(6¼[7]in)* from beg, ending with a P row.

Shape armholes
Cast off 3 sts at beg of next 2 rows and 2 sts at beg of foll 2 rows. **. 48[54] sts.

Divide for opening
Next row K2 tog, K22[25], turn and leave rem sts on holder. Complete this side first.
Next row K2, P to end.
Next row K2 tog, K to end. 22[25] sts.

2nd size only
Rep last 2 rows once more. 24 sts.

Both sizes
Keeping 2 sts at inside edge in g st, cont without shaping until armhole measures 11[12]cm *(4¼[4¾]in)* from beg, ending at armhole edge.

Shape shoulder and neck
Cast off at beg of next and every row 5 sts once, 4 sts once, 5 sts once and 4[5] sts twice.
With RS of work facing, rejoin yarn to rem sts, K to last 2 sts, K2 tog.
Next row P to last 2 sts, K2.
Complete to match first side.

Front
Work as given for back to **. Dec one st at each end of next and foll 1[2] alt rows. 44[48] sts. Cont without shaping until armholes measure 7[8]cm *(2¾[3¼]in)* from beg, ending with a P row.

Shape neck
Next row K19[20], turn and leave rem sts on holder.
Complete this side first. Cast off 2 sts at beg of next row. Keeping armhole edge straight, dec one st at neck edge on every foll alt row until 14[15] sts rem. Cont without shaping until front measures same as back to shoulder, ending at armhole edge.

Shape shoulder
Cast off at beg of next and foll alt rows 5 sts twice and 4[5] sts once.
With RS of work facing, rejoin yarn to rem sts, cast off first 6[8] sts for front neck, K to end. Complete to match first side.

Sleeves
Using No.11 needles and A, cast on 35[39] sts. Work 5cm *(2in)* rib as given for back, ending with a 2nd row. Change to No.9 needles. Beg with a K row, cont in st st, inc one st at each end of 3rd and every foll 4th row until there are 49[53] sts. Cont without shaping until sleeve measures 16[18]cm *(6¼[7]in)* from beg, ending with a P row.

Shape top
Cast off 3 sts at beg of next 2 rows. Dec one st at each end of next and foll 4[6] alt rows, ending with a P row. Cast off at beg of next and every row 2 sts 12 times and 9 sts once.

Left top : Charming baby's jersey with a rounded shirt collar. Left below : Cross-over cardigan with contrast edging.

Collar right half
Using No.9 needles and A, cast on 21[23] sts. Beg with a K row, cont in st st, inc one st at beg of 3rd and foll 2 alt rows. 24[26] sts. Cont without shaping until work measures 4.5[5]cm *(1¾[2]in)* from beg. Cast off.

Edging
Using No.3.00 (ISR) hook, A and with RS of work facing work 2 rows dc round outer edge of collar. Break off A. Join in B.
Next row 1ch, *work 1tr inserting hook into next dc of first row, 1ch, miss 1dc, rep from * ending with last tr worked into last dc of first row. Fasten off.

Collar left half
Work as given for collar right half, reversing shaping.

To make up
Press under a damp cloth with a warm iron. Join shoulder seams. Set in sleeves. Join side and sleeve seams. Sew on collar with shaped edges meeting at centre front neck. Sew in zip. Press seams. If required, work embroidery using B as shown in photograph.

Cross~over cardigan with crochet edging

Sizes
To fit 46[51]cm *(18[20]in)* chest
Length to shoulder, 28[32]cm *(11[12½]in)*
Sleeve seam, 18[20]cm *(7[7¾]in)*
The figures in brackets [ ] refer to the 51cm *(20in)* size only

Tension
28 sts and 36 rows to 10cm *(3.9in)* over st st worked on No.10 needles

Materials
4[5] x 20grm balls Lister Easywash 4 ply in main shade, A
1 ball of contrast colour, B
One pair No.10 needles
One pair No.12 needles
One No.3.00 (ISR) crochet hook
4 buttons

Back
Using No.12 needles and A, cast on 65[73] sts.
1st row K1, *P1, K1, rep from * to end.
2nd row P1, *K1, P1, rep from * to end.
Rep these 2 rows until work measures 5cm *(2in)* from beg, ending with a 2nd row. Change to No.10 needles. Beg with a K row, work 44[52] rows st st.

Shape raglans
**Next row K2, K2 tog, K to last 4 sts, sl 1, K1, psso, K2.
Next row P to end. **.
Rep last 2 rows until 25[29] sts rem, ending with a P row. Cast off.

Left front
Using No.12 needles and A, cast on 65[73] sts. Work 5cm *(2in)* rib as given for back, ending with a 2nd row. Change to No.10 needles.
Next row K to last 4 sts, K2 tog, K2.
Next row P to end.
Rep last 2 rows 21[25] times more. 43[47] sts.

Shape raglan
Next row K2, K2 tog, K to last 4 sts, K2 tog, K2.
Next row P to end.
Rep last 2 rows 17[19] times more. 7 sts.
Next row K2, K3 tog, K2.
Next row P5.
Next row K1, K3 tog, K1.
Next row P3.
Cast off.

Right front
Using No.12 needles and A, cast on 65[73] sts. Work 4 rows rib as given for back.
Next row (buttonhole row) Rib 3, cast off 3, rib to last 6 sts, cast off 3, rib to end.
Next row Rib to end, casting on 3 sts over those cast off in previous row.
Cont in rib until 4 rows less than on left front. Rep 2 buttonhole rows. Rib 2 more rows. Change to No.10 needles.
Next row K2, sl 1, K1, psso, K to end.
Next row P to end.
Rep last 2 rows 21[25] times more.

Shape raglan
Next row K2, sl 1, K1, psso, K to last 4 sts, sl 1, K1, psso, K2.
Next row P to end.
Rep last 2 rows 17[19] times more. 7 sts.
Next row K2, sl 1, K2 tog, psso, K2.
Next row P5.
Next row K1, sl 1, K2 tog, psso, K1.
Next row P3. Cast off.

Sleeves
Using No.12 needles and A, cast on 43[47] sts. Work 5cm *(2in)* rib as given for back, ending with a 2nd row and inc 10 sts evenly across last row. 53[57] sts. Change to No.10 needles. Beg with a K row, cont in st st until sleeve measures 18[20]cm *(7[7¾]in)* from beg, ending with a P row.

Shape raglans
Rep from ** to ** on back armhole shaping until 13 sts rem, ending with a P row. Cast off.

To make up
Press under a damp cloth with a warm iron. Join raglan seams. Join side and sleeve seams.
Edging Using No.3.00 (ISR) hook, A and with RS of work facing, beg at lower edge of right front and work 1 row dc up right front, round neck and down left front. Fasten off A. Using B and with RS of work facing, return to lower edge of right front and work another row dc, then 1 row crab st (ie. work in dc from left to right instead of right to left). Fasten off.
Press seams. Sew on buttons to correspond with buttonholes.

Jumpsuit with striped sleeves

Sizes
To fit 46[51]cm *(18[20]in)* chest
Length from back neck to crutch, 37[41]cm *(14½[16¼]in)*
Inside leg seam, 25[28]cm *(9¾[11]in)*
Sleeve seam, 19[21]cm *(7½[8¼]in)*
The figures in brackets [ ] refer to the 51cm *(20in)* size only
Tension
24 sts and 32 rows to 10cm *(3.9in)* over st st worked on No.9 needles
Materials
8[9] x 25grm balls Hayfield Gaylon Double Knitting in main shade, A
2[2] balls of contrast colour, B
One pair No.9 needles
One pair No.11 needles
One No.3.00 (ISR) crochet hook
25[30]cm *(10[12]in)* zip fastener

Right leg
Using No.9 needles and B, cast on 63[69] sts. ** K 4 rows with B. Beg with a K row, work 4 rows st st with A. **. Rep from ** to ** 3 times more. Break off B. Cont in st st with A until work measures 25[28]cm *(9¾[11]in)* from beg, ending with a P row.
Shape crutch
Dec one st at beg of next 5 rows, ending with a K row. 58[64] sts. Leave sts on holder.

Left leg
Work as given for right leg, reversing shaping by ending with a K row before shaping crutch.
Join legs
Next row P to last st, P last st tog with first st of right leg, P to end. 115[127] sts. Cont without shaping until work measures 22[25]cm *(8¾[9¾]in)* from beg of crutch shaping, ending with a P row.
Divide for armholes
Next row K26[29], K2 tog, K1, turn and leave rem sts on holder.
Complete right front first. Cont to dec one st at armhole edge as shown on every foll 4th row 4 times more, then on every foll alt row 5[7] times, ending with a P row. 19[20] sts.
Shape neck
Cast off at beg of next and foll alt rows, 3[4] sts once, 2 sts twice and one st twice, *at the same time* cont to dec at armhole edge as before until 3 sts rem. Cast off.

Two more practical playsuits for garden or beach. Far left: Jumpsuit with stripey sleeves and bell bottoms; left: sleeveless, V-neck playsuit with short trousers.

With RS of work facing, rejoin yarn to next st, K1, sl 1, K1, psso, K51[57], K2 tog, K1, turn and leave rem sts on holder. Cont on these sts for back. Dec one st as shown at each end of every foll 4th row 4 times more, then at each end of every foll alt row 12[14] times, ending with a P row. Leave rem 23[25] sts on holder.
With RS of work facing, rejoin yarn to next st, K1, sl 1, K1, psso, K to end. Complete left front to match right front.

Sleeves
Using No.11 needles and A, cast on 37[41] sts.
1st row (RS) K1, *P1, K1, rep from * to end.
2nd row P1, *K1, P1, rep from * to end.
Rep last 2 rows until work measures 5cm *(2in)* from beg, ending with a 2nd row. Change to No.9 needles. Join in B. Cont in patt throughout as given from ** to ** of right leg, inc one st at each end of 3rd and every foll 8th row until there are 47[51] sts. Cont without shaping until sleeve measures 19[21]cm *(7½[8¼]in)* from beg, ending with a WS row.
Shape top
Cont in patt, dec one st as given for back armhole shaping at each end of next and foll 4th row, then at each end of every foll alt row 18[20] times. Leave rem 7 sts on holder.

Neckband
Join raglan seams. Using No.11 needles, A and with RS of work facing, K up 11[12] sts up right front neck, K across sts of right sleeve, back neck and left sleeve, K2 tog at each back raglan seam, then K up 11[12] sts down left front neck. 57[61] sts. Beg with a 2nd row, work 6cm *(2¼in)* rib as given for sleeves. Cast off loosely in rib.

To make up
Press under a damp cloth with a warm iron. Join sleeve seams. Join inside leg and crutch seams. Fold neckband in half to inside and sl st in position. Using No.3.00 (ISR) hook and A, work 2 rows dc up each side of front opening. Sew in zip, joining rem part of front seam below zip. Press seams.

Sleeveless V-neck suit

Size
To fit 46[51]cm *(18[20]in)* chest
Length from back neck to crutch, 37[41]cm *(14½[16¼]in)*
Inside leg seam, 6cm *(2¼in)*
The figures in brackets [ ] refer to the 51cm *(20in)* size only
Tension
22 sts and 44 rows to 10cm *(3.9in)* over g st worked on No.8 needles
Materials
2[3] x 25grm balls Hayfield Beaulon Double Knitting in main shade, A
2[2] balls each of contrast colours, B, C, D
One pair No.8 needles
One No.3.00 (ISR) crochet hook
20cm *(8in)* zip fastener

Legs
Using No.8 needles and A, cast on 55[61] sts.
1st row (RS) K1, *P1, K1, rep from * to end.
2nd row P1, *K1, P1, rep from * to end.
Rep last 2 rows twice more. Cont in g st and stripe sequence throughout of 4 rows each of B, C, D and A, inc one st at each end of 3rd and every foll 6th row until there are 61[67] sts. Cont without shaping until work measures 6cm *(2¼in)* from beg, ending with a WS row.
Shape crutch
Cast off 3 sts at beg of next 2 rows. 55[61] sts. Leave sts on holder.
Work another leg in the same way, but do not leave sts on holder.
Join legs
Next row K to last st, K last st tog with first st of other leg, K to end. 109[121] sts. Cont in patt without shaping until work measures 23[26] cm *(9[10¼]in)* from join, ending with a WS row.
Divide for armholes
Next row K2 tog, K26[29], turn and leave rem sts on holder.
Complete right front first. Cast off at beg of next and foll alt rows 3 sts once, 2 sts once and one st 2[3] times, *at the same time* dec one st at front edge on every foll 6th row until 11[12] sts rem. Cont without shaping until armhole measures 14[15]cm *(5½[6]in)* from beg, ending at armhole edge.
Shape shoulder
Cast off at beg of next and foll alt rows 4 sts twice and 3[4] sts once.
With RS of work facing, rejoin yarn to next st, K53[59], turn and leave rem sts on holder. Cont on these sts for back. K 1 row. Cast off at beg of next and every row 3 sts twice, 2 sts twice and one st 4[6] times. 39[43] sts. Cont without shaping until armholes match front to shoulder, ending with a WS row.
Shape shoulders
Cast off at beg of next and every row 4 sts 4 times and 3[4] sts twice. Cast off rem 17[19] sts.
With RS of work facing, rejoin yarn to next st, K to last 2 sts, K2 tog tbl. Complete left front to match right front.

To make up
Do not press. Join shoulder seams. Join leg and crutch seams. Using No.3.00 (ISR) hook and A, work 2 rows dc round front edges, neck and armholes. Sew in zip, joining rem part of front below zip.

Trim trousers & jersey set

Size
Jersey to fit 51cm *(20in)* chest
Length to shoulder, 26.5cm *(10½in)*
Sleeve seam, 15cm *(6in)*
Trousers waist to crutch, 16cm *(6¼in)*
Inside leg seam, 28cm *(11in)*

Tension
32 sts and 42 rows to 10cm *(3.9in)* over st st worked on No.12 needles

Materials
3 x 50grm balls Mademoiselle Pingouin in main shade, A
2 balls of contrast colour, B
One pair No.12 needles
6 buttons
Waist length of 2.5cm *(1in)* wide elastic

Jersey front
Using No.12 needles and A, cast on 84 sts. Work 3cm *(1¼in)* K1, P1 rib. Break off A. Join in B. Beg with a K row, cont in st st until work measures 15cm *(6in)* from beg, ending with a P row. **.

Shape raglan
Cast off 3 sts at beg of next 2 rows. Dec one st at each end of next and every foll alt row until 38 sts rem. Work one row. Cast off.

Jersey back
Work as given for jersey front to **.

Shape raglan
Cast off 2 sts at beg of next 2 rows. Dec one st at each end of next and every foll alt row until 36 sts rem. Work 1 row. Cast off.

Right sleeve
Using No.12 needles and A, cast on 50 sts. Work 3cm *(1¼in)* K1, P1 rib. Break off A. Join in B. Beg with a K row, cont in st st, inc one st at each end of 5th and every foll 6th row until there are 62 sts. Cont without shaping until sleeve measures 15cm *(6in)* from beg, ending with a P row.

Shape raglan
Cast off 2 sts at beg of next 2 rows. Dec one st at each end of next and every foll alt row until 24 sts rem. Work one row, ending with a P row.

Shape neck
Next row Cast off 4 sts, K to last 2 sts, K2 tog.
Next row P to end.
Rep last 2 rows 3 times more. Cast off.

Left sleeve
Work as given for right sleeve, reversing neck shaping by ending with a K row when 24 sts rem.

Front border and neckband
Using No.12 needles, A and with RS of work facing, beg at 1.5cm *(½in)* in from beg of left front raglan and K up 40 sts to corner, 3 sts from corner st, 28 sts across front neck, 3 sts from corner st and 40 sts down right front raglan to within 1.5cm *(½in)* of beg of shaping. 114 sts. Work one row K1, P1 rib.
Next row (buttonhole row) Rib 14, cast off 3 sts, (rib 10, cast off 3 sts) twice, rib 28, cast off 3 sts, (rib 10, cast off 3 sts) twice, rib 14.
Next row Rib to end, casting on 3 sts over those cast off in previous row.
Work 3 more rows rib. Cast off in rib.

To make up
Press under a dry cloth with a cool iron. Join back raglans. Join front raglans for 1.5cm *(½in)* only. Join side and sleeve seams. Sew side edges of front border to sleeves.
Back neckband Using No.12 needles, A and with RS of work facing, beg at front shoulder of right sleeve and K up 62 sts evenly along top of sleeves and back to front shoulder of left sleeve. Work 6 rows K1, P1 rib. Cast off in rib.
Press seams. Sew 3 buttons on to each front sleeve raglan to correspond with buttonholes.

Trousers left leg
Using No.12 needles and A, cast on 88 sts. Beg with a K row, cont in st st until work measures 22cm *(8¾in)* from beg, ending with a P row.

Shape leg
Inc one st at each end of next and every foll 4th row until there are 100 sts, then at each end of every foll alt row until there are 104 sts. Cont without shaping until work measures 29cm *(11½in)* from beg, ending with a P row.

Shape crutch
Cast off at beg of next and every row 2 sts 4 times and one st 8 times, then cast off one st at beg of every foll 8th row twice. 86 sts. Cont without shaping until work measures 45cm *(17¾in)* from beg, ending with a P row.

Shape back
Next row K70 sts, turn.
Next row Sl 1, P to end.
Next row K54 sts, turn.
Next row Sl 1, P to end.
Next row K38 sts, turn.
Next row Sl 1, P to end.
Work 10 rows st st across all sts. Cast off.

Right leg
Work as given for left, reversing shaping.

To make up
Press as given for jersey. Join front and back seams from waist to crutch. Join inside leg seams. Turn 1.5cm *(½in)* hem at lower edge of legs to WS and sl st in position. Turn hem at waist edge to WS and sl st in position, enclosing elastic. Press seams.

A trim trouser suit to knit with buttoned raglan sleeves.

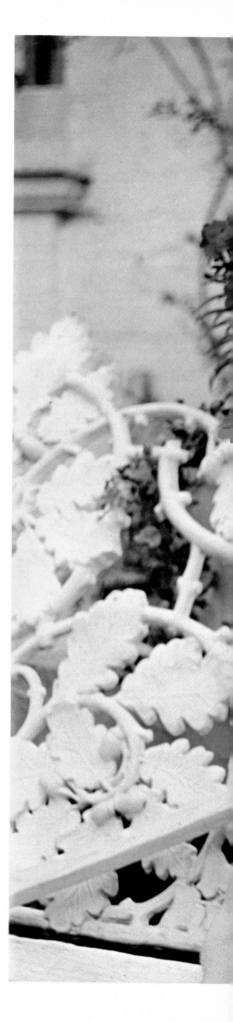

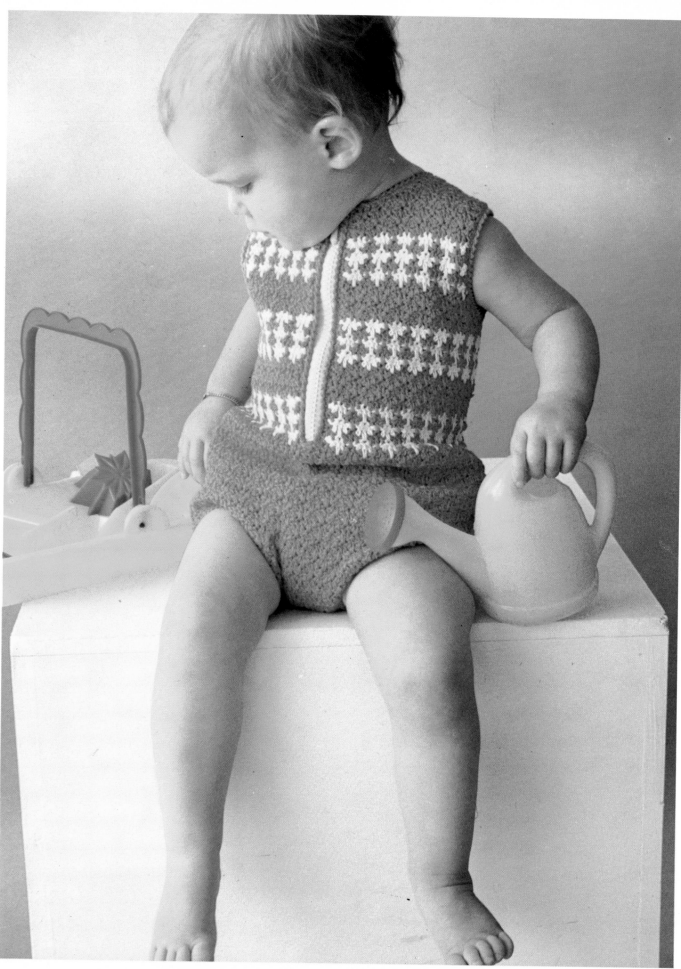

Sleeveless romper suit to crochet with daisy design

Sizes
To fit 51cm (*20in*) chest
Length from back neck to crutch, 43cm (*17in*)

Tension
20 sts to 9cm (*3½in*) and 10 rows to 7cm (*2¾in*) over patt worked on No.3.00 (ISR) hook

Materials
3 x 50grm balls Twilleys Stalite in main shade, A
1 ball of contrast colour, B
One No.3.00 (ISR) crochet hook
18cm (*7in*) zip fastener

Back
Using No.3.00 (ISR) hook and A, make 21ch and beg at crutch.
1st row (RS) Into 4th ch from hook work 1tr, 1tr into next ch, *1ch, miss 1ch, 1tr into each of next 3ch, rep from * to end. Turn. 19 sts.
2nd row 4ch to count as first tr and 1ch, *miss next tr, 1tr into next tr, yrh, insert hook into missed st on previous row, yrh and draw up a loop to same height as row being worked, finish as for an ordinary tr – called 1 long tr –, 1tr into next tr, 1ch, rep from * to end, finishing with miss next tr, 1tr into 3rd of 3ch. Turn.
3rd row 6ch, into 4th ch from hook work 1tr, 1tr into next ch, 1ch, miss 1ch, 1tr into next tr, * 1 long tr into missed st of previous row, 1tr into next tr, 1ch, miss 1tr, 1tr into next tr, rep from * to end, finishing with 1 long tr, 1tr into 3rd of 4ch. Turn. 23 sts.
4th row 7ch, into 6th ch from hook work 1tr, 1tr into next ch, 1tr into next tr, *1ch, miss 1tr, 1tr into next tr, 1 long tr into missed st of previous row, 1tr into next tr, rep from * to end, finishing with 1ch, miss 1 tr, 1tr into turning ch. Turn. 27 sts.
5th row 10ch, into 4th ch from hook work 1tr, 1tr into next ch, 1ch, miss 1ch, 1tr into each of next 3ch, 1ch, miss 1ch, 1tr into next tr, patt to end. Turn. 35 sts.
6th row 11ch, into 6th ch from hook work 1tr, 1tr into each of next 2ch, 1ch, miss 1ch, 1tr into each of next 2ch, 1tr into next tr, patt to end.

The discerning baby won't object to this nifty sleeveless romper suit to crochet. It has three bands of daisies cleverly worked into the design in a contrast colour, it has a convenient zip fastener at the front, and plenty of room for bulky nappies inside!

Turn. 43 sts.
Rep 5th and 6th rows twice more. 75 sts.
Cont in patt, dec one st at each end of 2nd and every foll alt row until 59 sts rem. Patt 2 rows, ending with a WS row. **. Cont in patt without shaping and in stripe sequence of (1 row B and 1 row A) twice, 1 row B, 5 rows A, (1 row B and 1 row A) twice, 1 row B and 2 rows A, ending with as RS row.
Break off B.
Shape armholes
Next row Ss over first 3 sts, patt to last 3 sts, turn.
Next row Ss over first 2 sts, patt to last 2 sts, turn.
Dec one st at each end of next row. 47 sts.
Cont without shaping and in stripe sequence of (1 row B and 1 row A) twice and 1 row B. Cont in A only until armholes measure 13cm (*5in*) from beg.
Next row Working into missed sts as they occur, 1ch, 1dc into each of next 3 sts, 1htr into each of next 4 sts, 1tr into each of next 31 sts, 1htr into each of next 4 sts, 1dc into each of last 4 sts. Fasten off.

Front
Work as given for back to **.
Divide for opening
Next row Patt over first 29 sts, turn. Complete this side first. Cont to match back to underarm, ending at centre front edge.
Shape armhole
Next row Patt to last 3 sts, turn.
Next row Ss over first 2 sts, patt to end. Turn.
Dec one st at end of next row. 23 sts. Cont in patt to match back until work measures 18cm (*7in*) from beg of opening, ending at armhole edge.
Shape neck
Next row Patt to last 5 sts, turn.
Next row Ss over first 3 sts, patt to end. Turn.
Dec one st at neck edge on next 3 rows. 12 sts. Cont without shaping until armhole matches back to shoulder, ending at armhole edge.
Next row 1ch, 1dc into each of next 3 sts, 1htr into each of next 4 sts, 1tr into each of next 4 sts.
Fasten off.
Return to where work was left, miss first st at centre front, rejoin yarn to next st and patt to end.
Complete to match other side.

To make up
Press under a damp cloth with a warm iron. Join shoulder, side and crutch seams. Using No.3.00 (ISR) hook, A and with RS of work facing, work a row of dc up right front edge, round neck and down left front, then work a row of crab st (ie. work in dc from left to right instead of from right to left). Work in the same way round legs and armholes.
Sew in zip. Press seams.

Layette with chevron design

Photograph overleaf
Sizes
To fit 46cm (*18in*) chest
Jacket length to shoulder, 28cm (*11in*)
Sleeve seam, 16cm (*6¼in*)
Jersey length to shoulder, 23cm (*9in*)
Sleeve seam, 4cm (*1½in*)

Tension
28 sts and 44 rows to 10cm (*3.9in*) over patt worked on No.10 needles

Materials
Emu Treasure Ripple Quickerknit
Complete set 17 x 20grm balls
Jacket 6 balls
Jersey 4 balls
Pull-ons 6 balls
Bonnet 1 ball
Bootees 1 ball
One pair No.10 needles
Set of 4 No.10 needles pointed at both ends
One No.3.00 (ISR) crochet hook
1 button for jacket
4 buttons for pull-ons

Jacket back and fronts
Using No.10 needles cast on 149 sts and work in one piece to underarm. Commence patt.
1st row (RS) K1, P3, *K9, P3, rep from * to last st, K1.
2nd and every alt row K4, *P9, K3, rep from * to last st, K1.
3rd row K1, P3, *yon, sl 1, K1, psso, K5, K2 tog, yrn, P3, rep from * to last st, K1.
5th row K1, P3, *K1, yfwd, sl 1, K1, psso, K3, K2 tog, yfwd, K1, P3, rep from * to last st, K1.
7th row K1, P3, *K2, yfwd, sl 1, K1, psso, K1, K2 tog, yfwd, K2, P3, rep from * to last st, K1.
9th row K1, P3, *K3, yfwd, sl 1, K2 tog, psso, yfwd, K3, P3, rep from * to last st, K1.
10th row As 2nd.
These 10 rows form patt. Rep them 6 times more.
Divide for armholes
Next row Patt 38, turn and leave rem sts on holder.
Complete right front first.
Next row Patt to end.
Next row Patt to last 3 sts, K2 tog, K1.
Rep last 2 rows 9 times more. 28 sts. Patt 7 rows, ending with a WS row.
Shape neck
Keeping armhole edge straight, cast off at beg of next and foll alt rows 5 sts once, 4 sts once and 2 sts once. Dec one st at beg of foll 4 alt rows. 13 sts. Patt 10 rows, ending with a RS row.
Shape shoulder
Cast off at beg of next and foll alt rows 4 sts twice and 5 sts once.
With RS of work facing, rejoin yarn to rem

sts, K2 tog, patt 69, K2 tog, turn and leave rem sts on holder. Cont on these sts for back.

**Next row Patt to end.

Next row K1, sl 1, K1, psso, patt to last 3 sts, K2 tog, K1.

Rep last 2 rows 9 times more. **. 51 sts. Cont without shaping until back matches front to shoulder, ending with a WS row.

Shape shoulders

Cast off at beg of next and every row 4 sts 4 times and 5 sts twice. Cast off rem 25 sts. With RS of work facing, rejoin yarn to rem sts and patt to end. Cont on these sts for left front.

Next row Patt to end.

Next row K1, sl 1, K1, psso, patt to end. Complete to match right front, reversing shaping as shown.

Sleeves

Using No.10 needles cast on 61 sts. Commence patt.

1st row P2, *K9, P3, rep from * to last 11 sts, K9, P2.

Cont in patt as given for back, keeping row ends as set, until 71 rows have been completed from beg.

Shape top

Rep from ** to ** as given for back armhole shaping. Cast off rem 41 sts.

To make up

Press under a damp cloth with a cool iron. Join shoulder seams. Join sleeve seams. Set in sleeves.

Edging Using No.3.00 (ISR) hook and with RS of work facing, work in dc all round outer edge. Join with a ss into first dc.

Next round 1ch, *into next dc work (1dc, 3ch and 3tr), miss 3dc, rep from * all round. Join with a ss into first ch. Fasten off.

Work a similar edging round lower edge of sleeves. Press seams.

Jersey back

Using No.10 needles cast on 73 sts.

1st row K1, *P1, K1, rep from * to end.

2nd row P1, *K1, P1, rep from * to end. Rep these 2 rows until work measures 2cm (¾in) from beg, ending with a 2nd row. Cont in patt as given for jacket sleeves until 61 rows have been worked in patt.

Shape armholes

Rep from ** to ** as given for jacket back armhole shaping. 53 sts. Leave sts on holder.

Front

Work as given for back.

Sleeves

Using No.10 needles cast on 49 sts. Work 2cm (¾in) rib as given for back. Cont in patt as given for back, work 11 rows.

Shape top

Rep from ** to ** as given for jacket back armhole shaping. 29 sts. Leave sts on holder.

Yoke

Using set of 4 No.10 needles and with RS of work facing, K across sts of back, first sleeve, front and second sleeve, K2 tog at each seam. 160 sts.

Next round *P1, K1, P1, K2 tog, rep from * to end. 128 sts.

Work 4cm (1½in) in rounds of K1, P1 rib.

Next round *Yfwd, K2 tog, rep from * to end.

Rib 1 more round. Cast off loosely in rib.

To make up

Press as given for jacket, omitting ribbing. Join raglan seams. Join side and sleeve seams. Make a twisted cord approx 66cm (26in) long and thread through holes at neck.

Pull-ons back

Using No.10 needles cast on 61 sts and work downwards from waist. Rib 4 rows as given for jersey back.

Next row K1, *yfwd, K2 tog, rep from * to end.

Rib 5 more rows, inc 15 sts evenly across last row. 76 sts. Cont in g st until work measures 17cm (6¾in) from beg, ending with a RS row.

Divide for legs

Next row K34, cast off 8, K to end. Cont on last 34 sts for right leg. Dec one st at inside edge on every foll 4th row until 20 sts rem. Cont without shaping until work measures 12cm (4¾in) from beg of legs, ending with a WS row. Leave sts on holder.

With RS of work facing, rejoin yarn to rem sts and complete other leg to match first leg.

Front

Work as given for back.

Left foot

Using No.10 needles and with RS of work facing, K across 20 sts from front leg, then 20 sts from back leg, K2 tog at seam. 39 sts.

Beg with a 2nd row, rib 3 rows as given for jersey back.

Next row K1, *yfwd, K2 tog, rep from * to end.

Rib 3 more rows. K 2 rows. **.

Next row K15, turn.

Next row K10, turn.

K 20 rows on these 10 sts. Break off yarn. Rejoin yarn to inside edge of 5 sts that were left, K up 10 sts along side of foot, K10, K up 10 sts along other side of foot, then K24. 59 sts. K 20 rows. Cast off.

Right foot

Work as given for left foot to **.

Next row K34, turn.

Next row K10, turn.

Complete to match left foot, rejoining yarn at inside edge of 24 sts after working foot.

Bodice back

Using No.10 needles and with RS of work facing, K up 51 sts from 61 cast on sts.

Commence patt.

Next row K3, *P9, K3, rep from * to end. Beg with a 3rd row and keeping row ends as set, patt 8 more rows as given for jacket back, ending with a WS row.

Next row K1, (pick up loop lying between needles and K tb1 – called M1 –, K1) twice, patt 45, (K1, M1) twice, K1. 55 sts.

Next row K5, patt 45, K5.

Next row K5, sl 1, K1, psso, patt to last 7 sts, K2 tog, K5.

Next row K5, patt to last 5 sts, K5. Rep last 2 rows 8 times more. 37 sts. K 9 rows.

Divide for straps

Next row K8, cast off 21, K to end. Cont in g st on each set of 8 sts until strap measures 4cm (1½in). Cast off.

Bodice front

Work as given for bodice back.

To make up

Press patt sections only as given for jacket. Join side seams. Join inner leg and crutch seams. Join seam under foot. Sew 2 buttons to top of each back strap and make 2 loops on each front strap to correspond. Using 4 strands of yarn, make a twisted cord approx 80cm (31½in) long and thread through waist and 2 cords approx 50cm (19¾in) long to thread through ankles.

Bonnet

Using No.10 needles cast on 77 sts. Work 50 rows patt as given for jacket back, dec 6 sts evenly across last row. 71 sts. Cont in g st, K 2 rows.

Shape crown

Next row *K8, K2 tog, rep from * to last st, K1. 64 sts.

Next row K to end.

Next row *K7, K2 tog, rep from * to last st, K1. 57 sts.

Cont to dec in this way on every foll alt row until 8 sts rem. Break off yarn, thread through rem sts, draw up and fasten off.

Neck edging

Join back seam from centre of crown to beg of g st section. Using No.3.00 (ISR) hook and with RS of work facing, work a row of dc along neck edge, turn.

Next row 4ch to count as first tr and ch, *miss 1dc, 1tr into next dc, 1ch, rep from * ending with 1tr into last dc. Fasten off. Work edging as given for jacket round face edge. Using 4 strands of yarn, make a twisted cord approx 60cm (23½in) long and thread through holes at neck.

Bootees

Using No.10 needles cast on 46 sts and beg at sole. K 2 rows.

Next row K1, pick up loop lying between needles and K tbl – called M1 –, K21, M1, K2, M1, K21, M1, K1.

Next row K to end.

Next row K2, M1, K21, M1, K4, M1, K21, M1, K2.

Cont to inc in this way on every foll alt row until there are 66 sts.

Above : A delightful layette knitted in a chevron design. There's a short-sleeved top, all-in-one leggings and bib, prettily shaped jacket, a bonnet and bootees.

Next row K2 tog, K30, K2 tog, K30, K2 tog. 63 sts.
Beg with a 1st row, patt 10 rows as given for jacket sleeves, beg and end each row with 3 sts instead of 2 and inc 3 sts across

last row. 66 sts.
Next row K16 and leave these sts on holder, cast off 12, K10, turn.
K18 rows on 10 sts just worked. Break off yarn.
With RS of work facing, rejoin yarn to inner edge of rem 28 sts, cast off 12, K16.
Next row P16, P centre 10 sts, P across 16 sts from holder. 42 sts.
Next row K2 tog, *yfwd, K2 tog, rep from

* to end. 41 sts.
Next row P1, *K1, P1, rep from * to end.
Rib 3 more rows. Cast off in rib.

To make up
Join back seam. Join seams at side of top of foot. Work edging as given for jacket round top. Make twisted cords approx 50cm (19¾in) long to thread through ankles.

53

One-piece suit with long legs

Sizes
To fit 46[51]cm *(18[20]in)*
Length from back neck to crutch, 37[41]cm
(14½[16¼]in)
Inside leg seam, 25[28]cm *(9¾[11]in)*
Sleeve seam, 19[21]cm *(7½[8¼]in)*
The figures in brackets [ ] refer to the
51cm *(20in)* size only

Tension
28 sts and 36 rows to 10cm *(3.9in)* over st
st worked on No.10 needles

Materials
5[6] x 25 grm balls Patons Trident 4 ply
in main shade, A
2[3] balls of contrast colour, B
One pair No.10 needles
One pair No.12 needles
One No.2.50 (ISR) crochet hook
25[30]cm *(10[12]in)* zip fastener

Left leg
Using No.12 needles and A, cast on 51[57]
sts.
1st row K1, *P1, K1, rep from * to end.
2nd row P1, *K1, P1, rep from * to end.
Rep last 2 rows until work measures 4cm
(1½in) from beg, ending with a 2nd row.
Change to No. 10 needles. Beg with a K
row, cont in st st, inc one st at each end of
first and every foll 8th row until there are
71[79] sts. Cont without shaping until
work measures 25[28]cm *(9¾[11]in)* from
beg, ending with a P row. **.
Shape crutch
Dec one st at each end of next and foll alt
row, then one st at end only of foll alt row.
P 1 row. Leave rem 66[74] sts on holder.

Right leg
Work as given for left leg to **.
Shape crutch
Dec one st at each end of next and foll alt
row, then at beg only of foll alt row. P 1
row.
Join legs
Next row K to last st, K last st tog with
first st of left leg, K to end. 131[147] sts.
Cont without shaping until work measures
18[21] cm *(7[8¼]in)* from beg of crutch
shaping, ending with a P row. Join in B.
Work 4 rows B, 2 rows A, 6 rows B and 4
rows A. Break off A.
Divide for armholes
Next row Using B, K29[33], sl 1, K1,
psso, K2, turn and leave rem sts on holder.
Complete right front first. Dec one st at
armhole edge as shown on every 4th row
5[4] times more, then on every alt row
until 24[25] sts rem, ending with a P row.
Shape neck
Cont to dec at raglan as before, *at the same
time* cast off at beg of next and foll alt rows
3 sts once [twice], 2 sts 3[2] times and one st
3 times. Keeping neck edge straight, dec
at raglan edge only until 3 sts rem. Cast off.

With RS of work facing, rejoin yarn to rem
sts, K2, K2 tog, K57[65], sl 1, K1, psso,
K2, turn and leave rem sts on holder.
Complete back. Dec as shown at each end of
every foll 4th row 5[4] times more, then at
each end of every alt row until 29[31] sts
rem, ending with a P row. Leave sts on
holder.
With RS of work facing, rejoin yarn to rem
sts, K2, K2 tog, K to end. Complete left
front to match right front, reversing
shaping.

Sleeves
Using No.12 needles and A, cast on 47[51]
sts. Work 4cm *(1½in)* rib as given for left
leg, ending with a 2nd row. Change to
No.10 needles. Beg with a K row, cont in st
st, inc one st at each end of 5th and every
foll 8th row until there are 59[63] sts,
at the same time when sleeve measures
15[17]cm *(6[6¾]in)* from beg, ending with a
P row, cont in stripe sequence of 4 rows B,
2 rows A, 6 rows B and 4 rows A. Break
off A.
Shape top
Next row K2, K2 tog, K to last 4 sts, sl 1,
K1, psso, K2.
Next row P to end.
Rep last 2 rows until 11 sts rem, ending
with a P row. Leave sts on holder.

Neckband
Join raglan seams. Using No.12 needles, B
and with RS of work facing, K up 15[16]
sts up right front neck, K across sts of
right sleeve, back neck and left sleeve, K2
tog at each back raglan seam, K up 15[16]
sts down left front neck. 79[83] sts. Beg
with a 2nd row, work 5cm *(2in)* rib as
given for left leg. Cast off loosely in rib.

To make up
Press under a damp cloth with a warm iron.
Join sleeve seams. Join inside leg and
crutch seams. Fold neckband in half to
inside and sl st in position. Using No.2.50
(ISR) hook and A, work in dc up right
front edge, changing to B at beg of stripe
patt, cont up to neck, turn and work a
second row, changing colour again at beg
of stripes. Work left front edge to match.
Sew in zip to come to top of neck, then
join seam below zip. Press seams.

Simple dress with striped yoke

Sizes
To fit 51[56]cm *(20[22]in)* chest
Length, 30cm *(11¾in)*
Sleeve seam, 13cm *(5in)*

Tension
28 sts and 36 rows to 10cm *(3.9in)* over
st st worked on No.10 needles
Materials
5 x 25grm balls Patons Trident 4 ply in
main shade, A
1 ball of contrast colour, B
1 ball of contrast colour, C
One pair No.10 needles
One pair No.12 needles
One No.12 circular Twin-Pin
One No.2.50 (ISR) crochet hook
5 buttons

Back
Using No.12 needles and A, cast on 106 sts.
K 8 rows. Change to No.10 needles. Beg
with a K row, cont in st st, dec one st at
each end of 5th and every foll 12th row
until 96 sts rem. Cont without shaping
until work measures 19cm *(7½in)* from
beg, ending with a P row.
Shape armholes
Next row K1, K2 tog, K to last 3 sts,
sl 1, K1, psso, K1.
Next row P to end.
Rep last 2 rows 4 times more. **. 86 sts.
Leave sts on holder.

Front
Work as given for back.

Sleeves
Using No.12 needles and A, cast on 46 sts.
K 8 rows. Change to No.10 needles. Beg
with a K row, cont in st st, inc one st at
each end of first and every foll 8th row
until there are 56 sts. Cont without
shaping until sleeve measures 13cm *(5in)*
from beg, ending with a P row.
Shape top
Rep from ** to ** as given for back.
Leave rem 46 sts on holder.

Yoke
Join raglan seams. With RS of work facing,
sl first 43 sts of back on to holder, using
No.12 circular Twin-Pin, rejoin A to next
st, K40, sl 1, K1, psso, K last st of back tog
with first st of sleeve, cont across sleeve,
K2 tog, K to last 3 sts, sl 1, K1, psso, K
last st of sleeve tog with first st of front,
cont across all sts, dec as shown at each
seam. 252 sts. Cont in rows, with opening
at centre back.
Next row K to end.
Shape yoke
Cont in g st and stripe sequence of 4 rows
B, 6 rows C and 2 rows A, *at the same time*
shape yoke as foll:
1st row K1, (K2 tog, K2) 62 times, K2
tog, K1. 189 sts.
13th row K6, (K2 tog, K6) 22 times, K2
tog, K5. 166 sts.
25th row K5, (K2 tog, K5) 22 times, K2
tog, K5. 143 sts.
35th row K5, (K2 tog, K4) 22 times, K2
tog, K4. 120 sts.
43rd row K4, (K2 tog, K3) 22 times, K2
tog, K4. 97 sts.
51st row K4, (K2 tog, K2) 22 times, K2

tog, K3. 74 sts.
59th row K3, (K2 tog, K1) 22 times, K2

Below left : Form-fitting one-piece suit.
Below right : A simple dress with an effective striped yoke and raglan sleeves.

tog, K3. 51 sts.
Using A, K 6 rows.
Cast off.

To make up
Press under a damp cloth with a warm iron,

omitting yoke. Join side and sleeve seams. Using No.2.50 (ISR) hook and A, work 2 rows dc down each side of back opening, making 5 button loops of 3ch on right back edge (one at each stripe in A, top one at neck). Press seams. Sew on buttons.

Suntop & shorts for a small child

Sizes
Top to fit 51[56]cm *(20[22]in)* chest
Length approx 36[41]cm *(14¼[16¼]in)*
Shorts length at side, 24[26]cm
(9½[10¼]in)
The figures in brackets [ ] refer to the 56cm
(22in) size only
Tension
24 sts and 32 rows to 10cm *(3.9in)* over st
st worked on No.9 needles

*Lightweight sun tops for mother and child –
but a lucky little girl gets shorts to match
as well!*

Materials
Top 3[3] x 20grm balls Wendy Marina
Double Crepe in main shade, A
2[2] balls of contrast colour, B
Shorts 3[4] balls in main shade, A
One pair No.9 needles

One No.3.00 (ISR) crochet hook
2 buttons for top
Waist length of elastic for shorts

Top back
Using No.9 needles and A, cast on 60[66] sts. Beg with a K row, cont in st st and stripe sequence of 6 rows A and 6 rows B until 60[66] rows have been completed.
Shape armholes
Keeping stripes correct, cast off at beg of next and every row 3[5] sts twice, 2 sts 16 times and one st 6 times. Cast off.

Front
Work as given for back to underarm.
Shape armholes
Cast off at beg of next and every row 3[5] sts twice and 2 sts 15 times. 24[26] sts.
Shape neck
Next row (WS) Cast off 2 sts, P7, cast off 8[10] sts, P7.
Cont on last 7 sts. Dec one st at each end of next and foll alt row. P 1 row. K3 tog. Fasten off.
With RS of work facing, rejoin yarn to rem 7 sts and complete to match first side.

To make up
Press under a dry cloth with a cool iron. Join side seams.
Edging Using No.3.00 (ISR) hook, A and with RS of work facing, join yarn to top of left side seam, work in dc round front armhole edge, *make 25 [35]ch, turn, into 3rd ch from hook work 1dc, 1dc into each ch back to top of armhole, *, cont in dc round front neck, rep from * to *, then cont in dc down armhole and across back. Join with a ss into first dc.
Next round 1ch, 1dc into each dc up armhole, cont in dc along strap to end, make 5ch for button loop, cont in dc along other side of strap, round front neck, along second strap, make 5ch, then cont in dc along strap, down armhole and across back. Join with a ss into first ch. Fasten off.
Using No.3.00 (ISR) hook, A and with RS of work facing, work 1 row dc round lower edge. Press seams. Sew buttons to top of back.

Shorts right leg
Using No.9 needles and A, cast on 66[72] sts. Beg with a K row, cont in st st, inc one st at each end of every 3rd row until there are 74[80] sts. Work 2 more rows st st.
Shape crutch
Cast off at beg of next and every row 3 sts twice and 2 sts twice. Dec one st at end (back edge) of next and foll 2 alt rows. 61[67] sts. Cont without shaping until work measures 22[24]cm (8¾[9½]in) from beg, ending with a P row.
Next row K1, *P1, K1, rep from * to end.
Next row P1, *K1, P1, rep from * to end.
Rep last 2 rows 5 times more. Cast off loosely in rib.

Left leg
Work to match right leg, reversing shaping.

To make up
Press as given for top. Join front and back seams. Fold top ribbing in half to WS and sl st in position, leaving opening for elastic. Thread elastic through and secure. Work 1 row dc around lower edge of legs. Press seams.

Mother's sun top

Sizes
To fit 81.5[86.5:91.5]cm (32[34:36]in) bust
Length 61[62:63]cm (24[24½:24¾]in)
The figures in brackets [ ] refer to the 86.5 (34) and 91.5cm (36in) sizes respectively
Tension
24 sts and 32 rows to 10cm (3.9in) over st st worked on No.9 needles
Materials
6[7] x 20grm balls Wendy Marina Double Crepe in main shade, A
4[4] balls of contrast colour, B
One pair No.9 needles
One N.3.00 (ISR) crochet hook

Back
Using No.9 needles and A, cast on 96[102:108] sts. Beg with a K row, cont in st st and stripe sequence of 6 rows A and 6 rows B until 132[138:144] rows have been completed. **. Cast off.

Front
Work as given for back to **.
Shape armholes and divide for neck
Next row Cast off 4[5:6] sts, K until there are 43[45:47] sts on right hand needle, turn and leave rem sts on holder.
Complete this side first. Keeping stripes correct, dec one st at each end of every foll alt row until 3 sts rem, ending with a K row. Cast off.
With RS of work facing, rejoin yarn to sts on holder, cast off 2 sts, K to end.
Next row Cast off 4[5:6] sts, P to end. Complete to match first side.

Straps (make 2)
Using No.3.00 (ISR) hook and A, make 7ch.
Base row Into 3rd ch from hook work 1dc, 1dc into each ch to end. Turn. 6dc.
1st row 1ch to count as first dc, miss first st, 1dc into each dc to end. Turn.
Rep last row until strap measures 59.5cm (23½in) or length required. Fasten off.

To make up
Press under a dry cloth with a cool iron. Join side seams. Turn up 2 stripes at lower edge for hem and sl st in position. Using No.3.00 (ISR) hook and A, work 3 rounds dc around top edge. Stitch one strap to point at top of each side of front to tie at back neck. Press seams.

Cuddly duffel coat

Photograph overleaf
Sizes
To fit 51[56:61]cm (20[22:24]in) chest
Length to shoulder, 35.5[40.5:45.5]cm (14[16:18]in)
Sleeve seam, 16.5[20.5:24]cm (6½[8:9½]in)
The figures in brackets [ ] refer to the 56 (22) and 61cm (24in) sizes respectively
Tension
13 sts and 26 rows to 10cm (3.9in) over g st worked on No.2 needles
Materials
7[8:9] x 50grm balls Patons Husky Chunky Knitting
One pair No.2 needles
One pair No.4 needles
6 toggles
Press fastener
0.90 metre (1 yard) x 4cm (1½in) wide petersham ribbon

Back and fronts
Using No.2 needles cast on 95[103:113] sts and work in one piece to underarm. Cont in g st until work measures 15[19:23]cm (6[7½:9]in) from beg.
Next row (buttonhole row) K1, K2 tog, yfwd, K7[7:9], yfwd, K2 tog, K to end. K 17[19:21] rows.
Divide for back and front raglans
Next row K25[27:30] and leave these sts on holder, cast off 4, K until there are 37[41:45] sts on needle then leave these sts on holder, cast off 4, K to end.
Cont on last set of 25[27:30] sts for left front of girl's coat or right front of boy's coat. K 3 rows. Dec one st at beg of next and every foll 4th row until 21[23:26] sts rem, then at beg of every foll alt row until 17[18:20] sts rem, ending at front edge.
Shape neck
Next row Cast off 7[7:8] sts, K until there are 3 sts on needle and leave these sts on holder, K to end. 7[8:9] sts.
Dec one st at each end of next and foll 1[1:2] alt rows. Keeping neck edge straight, cont dec at raglan edge as before on foll 2[3:2] alt rows. K1 row. Fasten off.
Rejoin yarn to centre 37[41:45] sts on holder and cont on these sts for back. K 3 rows. Dec one st at each end of next and every foll 4th row until 29[33:37] sts rem, then at each end of every foll alt row until 13[13:15] sts rem. K 1 row. Leave sts on holder.
Rejoin yarn to rem 25[27:30] sts on holder and cont on these sts for right front of girl's coat or left front of boy's coat. K 1 row.
Next row (buttonhole row) K1, K2 tog, yfwd, K7[7:9], yfwd, K2 tog, K to end. K 1 row. Dec one st at end of next and every foll 4th row until 21[23:26] sts rem, then at end of every foll alt row until

19[20:22] sts rem. K1 row.

Next row (buttonhole row) K1, K2 tog, yfwd, K7[7:9], yfwd, K2 tog, K to last 2 sts, K2 tog.

Dec one st at end of foll alt row. 17[18:20] sts.

Shape neck

Next row K10[11:12], cast off rem 7[7:8] sts, fasten off, turn.

Next row Sl first 3 sts on to holder, rejoin yarn, K2 tog, K to last 2 sts, K2 tog. Complete to match first front.

Sleeves

Using No.4 needles cast on 25[27:29] sts. K 10 rows g st. Change to No.2 needles. Cont in g st, inc one st at each end of next and every foll 8th [10th:12th] row until there are 33[35:37] sts. Cont without shaping until sleeve measures 16.5[20.5:24]cm (*6½[8:9½]in*) from beg.

Shape raglan

Cast off 2 sts at beg of next 2 rows. K 2 rows. Dec one st at each end of next and every foll 4th row until 21[21:23] sts rem, then at each end of every alt row until 5 sts rem. K 1 row. Leave sts on holder.

Hood

Place a coloured thread on main part to mark RS of fabric with buttonholes to the right for girl's coat and to the left for boy's coat. Join raglan seams. Using No.4 needles and with RS of work facing, rejoin and K3 sts from holder on right front, K up 5[6:6] sts up front neck, K across 5 sleeve sts, 13[13:15] back neck sts, K across 5 sleeve sts, K up 5[6:6] sts down front neck and K across 3 sts on holder. 39[41:43] sts. K 6 rows g st.

Next row K9[10:11], pick up loop lying between needles and K tbl – called M1 –,

Two warm coats on a cool spring day, but only one of them is to knit! This cuddly duffel coat with hood can be made for boys and girls.

(K3, M1) 7 times, K9[10:11]. 47[49:51] sts.

Change to No.2 needles. Cont in g st until hood measures 18[19:20.5]cm (*7[7½:8]in*) from beg. Cast off 18 sts at beg of next 2 rows. 11[13:15] sts. Work a further 12.5cm (*5in*) on these sts. Cast off.

To make up

Join side edges of hood centre piece to cast off sts. Join sleeve seams. Sew on toggles to correspond with buttonholes and press fastener to neck edge. Face front edges with petersham ribbon and cut buttonholes to correspond with main fabric. Neaten buttonholes.